Truth & Light

brief explanations

His Holiness

M. R. Guru Bawa

Acknowledgements

Narrators:
   Lex Hixon—WBAI, New York
   Will Noffke—KQED, San Francisco

Translator:
   Prof. Mohammed Mauroof

Editors:
   Carolyn Pessolano
   Myrna Miller
   Crisi Rudnicki

Photographers:
   Wahvammah
   Carl Marcus
   Suvikash
   Jules Paz y Mino
   Terry Barnum
   Dr. Howard Posner

Production Editor:
   Rodger Hayne

Coordinating Editor:
   Mitchell Gilbert

First Printing: June 1974
Second Printing: February, 1980
Printed in the United States of America

Library of Congress Card Number: 74-76219
ISBN: Hardcover 0-914390-03-1
       Paperback 0-914390-04-x

Contents

Forward by Lex Hixon 5
Preface by Mitchell Gilbert 8

Interviews with Guru Bawa
    WBAI, June 17, 1973 11
    WBAI, October 14, 1973 39
    KQED, October 27, 1973 75
    WBAI, December 16, 1973 113

Foreword

Imagine the F.M. radios within a sixty-mile radius of New York City. Then imagine a human being who has been wandering through the Middle East, India, China, and Ceylon for the decades of our century and more, immersed in the experience of Ultimate Reality. Now bring the two images together: an experimental civilization of electronic media communication—and a primal civilization of holy life communion. The two make friends. As a result, countless dwellers in the super-city of the twentieth century feel within themselves the actual vibrations of an ancient sage, a sage totally untouched by commercial society, who is speaking from beyond the space and time of any society, a doorway between dimensions, a fountain of living water, freeing to the spirit, purifying to the mind, refreshing to the body, uncanny yet wholly natural.

Dialing at random across the F.M. band on Sunday morning. Patches of classical and contemporary music separated by hissing static. An occasional human voice transmits information. Then, at the listener-sponsored Pacifica station near the dial's center, we tune in a remarkable sound, a high-pitched, ecstatic bird-speech: the language is unrecognizable but is pervaded by a profound musicality and clarity. It is a secret song from the jungle of

Ceylon: the language is Tamil, the instrument is the voice of a being free from anger, desire, and death, a being full of tranquility, compassion, and life, a being who is called "Bawa," but who remains fundamentally beyond name and form. For this is the way Bawa is experienced over radio, as formless. The mellow voice of the translator now interrupts, giving our minds a sense of direction. Yet in the spiritual center of our consciousness, Bawa's voice rings alone, uninterrupted, like a bell or a stream, needing no translation. On and on flows the discourse: a symphony, a generous spring rain soaking into the thirsty core of our being. And now another voice is heard. That of an interviewer. A more familiar dimension is now added to the experience. Someone from

our civilization, a kind of tentative, sympathetic seeker and intellectual, is actually walking into the sacred space of this discourse to pose questions, questions a bright child might ask of its father or mother. "What does it feel like to be fully grown?" "Why did the earth begin?" There is no way this child can receive answers it will competely understand, but the interchange is refreshing, even touching.

I was that interviewer. I walked into that sacred space, that infinite space where, surrounded by microphones, a tiny human being with white beard, white turban, white clothing, and bright eyes smiled at me, spoke to me in a strange language, embraced me, placing his hand upon my forehead and my heart, opening doors of illumination, doors to the landscape where the Sun of Truth is forever shining. There was no crash of thunder, no flash of lightning, just a deepening of love and understanding, a ripening in gentle sunlight, in purity of heart. Countless sisters and brothers invisible to my eyes shared this spiritual experience with me over the radio. Not just with me but as me. It is in this feeling of oneness with my radio-family, oneness with my whole humanity-family, that I offer our gratitude at the shrine of Wisdom where Bawa sits, forever praising the Infinite.

Lex Hixon

Editor's Preface

The Truth itself is a vibration, an effulgence, a sound heard without ears, a light seen without eyes. From the beginning there have been those such as Guru Bawa who, having understood that Truth, had to find ways to reveal that which cannot be realized except through direct experience.

To the intellectual mind, it would seem impossible for that Truth to be conveyed in a book such as this. First, because the words attributed to Guru Bawa were originally spoken in an ancient language called Tamil. They were translated as they were spoken by Professor Mohamed Mauroof. Next, when the word-for-word transcript was examined, it became apparent that the vibration in Guru Bawa's voice transmitted meanings that simply were not as clear in printed form. So it became necessary for a small team of editors to work on the text.

Yet, as this book unfolded, it became increasingly certain that each reader could experience that Truth in the words printed on these pages. It became clear that the same One God out of whom that original Vibration comes is also the God within each of us who receives that Vibration and understands.

For example, in conversations after the fact, both Lex Hixon and Will Noffke talked about the special quality each experienced during their radio interviews of Guru Bawa. While both have long experience interviewing spiritual leaders on their programs, each found themselves asking questions as genuine seekers—not as professional radio personalities. Specific thanks should be given to the Pacifica radio network for seeking out and airing such interviews.

Professor Mauroof, who so graciously traveled to New York and to San Francisco in

order to translate for these programs, described the experience this way: "There really isn't any translating going on at a conscious or intellectual level. It is as though the explanation needed at that moment simply exploded inside of Guru Bawa and came out through His lips as a sound called Tamil. That sound explodes inside of me and comes out as a sound called English. So if that sound called English also explodes inside the listener, everyone has heard the same thing."

The editors had similar experiences. The Vibration edits itself just as surely as it allows itself to be heard as sound. When the eyes of one of the editors passed by a passage that needed greater clarity, the words would blur and the eyes automatically seemed to return to the previous sentence. Similarly, when the impulse came to make an intellectually-motivated change, the hand often became heavy and unable to write.

Undoubtedly, the reader will have similar experiences. That which most needs to be understood now, will make itself understood. At some later date, when more understanding is needed, the reader will return to this book and find exactly the meaning that is needed then.

As Guru Bawa has said, "It is God who sees God."

Mitchell Gilbert

Truth & Light

WBAI Radio
New York

Sunday morning
June 17, 1973

GURU BAWA

To my most loved children, to the children who are within love and who are most determined, to all of you, to all of the male children and to all of the female children, I express my most heartfelt love and greetings.

In this world, among all of the creations, among all of the various beings, I am the most lowly and the smallest one. There are not many things that I know about the various explanations of the world and its meanings. When I look at them, all of the creations of God seem to me to be greater in wisdom than I am. Among all the creations of God, I have not seen anything that is lowlier than myself. Like an ant or a fiber, I am very small and a slave of God. With compassion, I am a slave to all living beings. I am not educated. I have no titles. I am not a swami. I am not a guru. I am not a great person. I am very small and the very least in wisdom. These children have asked me to come here today, and it is not possible to disappoint them, so I have come.

Since I am not imbued with a great amount of education and a great amount of wisdom, there is a certain amount of tiredness and lack of courage felt. So if there are any mistakes in what is being said, either in the questions or in the answers, I seek your pardon.

LEX HIXON

You are listening to "In the Spirit." This

morning we have an unusual situation. We are in Studio C with about 100 people, and we have Guru Bawa with us, who is a teacher from Ceylon. He has been visiting this country, in Philadelphia. He is going to answer our questions and give a discourse, and perhaps he will also sing. Mohamed Mauroof is going to be our translator this morning, as Guru Bawa speaks in Tamil.

Guru Bawa, in our culture, today is Father's Day, and we wish you from our hearts a happy Father's Day!

GURU BAWA

We are all here, and God is Father to us all. For all creation, for all beings, God is Father. He has many names, many kinds of appellation; there are many ways of describing Him, but He is the one Father for all beings. He is the One who conducts creation, sustenance, and protection. Even in those situations where our parents forget us, He is always protecting us without ever forgetting. So it is to God, our Father, that we should all pay our obeisance and respects. In this world, among the different forms of life, we find different individuals performing their duties as fathers and mothers. But they are all of one family, and the Father of that family is One God. All of us, the creations, are like a funny family of God—a funny and interesting sort of family. Let all of us in this family, this funny family, let us, all together, pay our well wishes and respects to

13

our Father today.

LEX HIXON
Guru Bawa, your children spontaneously call you Father *(Bawa)*. What is the relationship between you as father and God as Father?

GURU BAWA
It is like the relationship between the sun and the earth. In the same way that there is a relationship between the sun and the earth, there is that relationship between His Truth and His slaves, the slaves of God. And in this same way there is the relationship between God and His children. So it is God who is the Father. We are not the Father.

There are two points here. Anything that disappears cannot be our true Father, since that thing can be destroyed. But that which does not disappear, that which is present forever, *That* is the Father. To a certain extent, there is His Treasure and His Wisdom within us. And there is a duty to bestow that Wealth, that Wisdom, on others. But other than that, we are not accepting the other burden.

LEX HIXON
Bawa, when we look at you we see an ordinary human being, but is there anything within you except God and the Qualities of God?

GURU BAWA
For us, as well as for the children, the sec-

tion known as the body is the earth, the fire, the water, the air, and the ether. This is something that everyone can see. Yet within this, there is another Mystery. That Mystery is something that cannot be discovered by any means, not even by the power of the atom. It is not something that can be discovered by science. It is a Power that is without form or image. It has no color; It has no hues. It has no race; It has no religion. It does not recognize differences. It is a Power of this sort that is within the human being. And whoever it is within whom that Power manifests, once he sees that Power, he will never keep anything other than that Power within himself. One who has seen that Power will not keep within him anything other than that. This is the one secret, and that is what he has with him.

LEX HIXON

Guru Bawa, can you tell us a brief account of your personal history, or is personal history not important to you?

GURU BAWA

What personal history can we speak about? What can we say? This is a school; it is like a university. There are so many creations in this, so many beings of God from whom we can learn. From whatever we see, from the ant that crawls, to the sun and the moon and all things beyond that, there are things to be learned. In everything, there are things for a student to

15

learn. Everything is a wonder! There are so many colors, so many wisdoms, so many examples. What colors! What wonders! When we have to learn from all of the wonders of God, are we to write of the history of the one who is studying? What is the point? It is the history of the One who created all of these wonders that we should be concerned about. That is the True History. The history of the student is not the lasting word.

LEX HIXON
Guru Bawa, are you going to be reborn again into this school, or have you graduated from this school?

GURU BAWA
I am not here to be born again. But I will not say that I have been graduated. I have not finished.

LEX HIXON
People in the audience may be wishing to ask a question of the Guru. We have a hand microphone which will be passed to the person asking. So raise your hand if you have a question.

FIRST QUESTIONER
Guru Bawa, could you please tell me which is more important, faith or meditation? Which do you advocate, faith or meditation?

GURU BAWA
Without a fire, you cannot cook. Like that,

what a human being needs first of all is a strong faith. That strength is his first requirement. Secondly, a human being needs the Qualities of God, that Love. The third requirement for a human being is His Conscience. He must understand that the lives of others are the same as his own. He must realize this within his conscience. Fourth, even if he still sees differences, he must have Forbearance and Patience. Having received the Beauty of that Patience and Forbearance, then he must receive and utilize the Wisdom of God.

As the first requirement, the first inspiration, the first cause, it is absolutely necessary to have faith, determination, and certitude. Without the Qualities of God, without having the Divine Qualities of patience, tolerance, and peacefulness, how can we worship or meditate upon God? It would be like trying to take water from a pond without a vessel to take it in. It would be like looking for light in a house where there is no light.

SECOND QUESTIONER

Do you think that it is possible to live in a place such as New York City and attain spiritual satisfaction?

GURU BAWA

There is no place where there is no world, where there is no illusion, where there is no torpor. There is no place where there are no animals, where there are no demons, where there are no satans, where there are no evil spirits and magics. All the scenes we see outside with our senses also exist within us, within the body. The essence of the beings of 18,000 universes exists within the body in a formless state. All of it is within this body. Within the body are the demons, the spirits, the lion, the tiger, the snake and the eagle, the peacock and all of the birds. All things are located here within the body itself. When all of these things are kept within us, what need is there to go to another city or country? Therefore, going here or there is not necessary. We must destroy the forest here within us and distill this ocean of illusion that exists within. We must catch and chain this monkey of the mind. There are 70 battalions of monkeys within this mind! And there is a huge dog of desire within us, and there is magic and torpor and illusion. In the body, below the waist there are seven hells, and above, in the upper part of the body, there are eight heavens. What is known as this world is this. [Points to the chest.] The mind is the world. This mind is the world. If you look (down) from the uppermost point, the mind is the eighth sphere. And if you look (up) from the lowermost point, the mind is the eighth sphere or world.

But, my children, do not worship asking for heaven, and do not cry asking that you be saved from hell. If you reflect and think and look within yourself and know what you are, then you will realize that wherever it is that you live, wherever it is that you reside, wherever it is that your mind travels, wherever it is that your mind goes to seek solace in the darkness, whatever house the dog of your desire is guarding, and wherever it is that your mind, your intelligence, your wisdom, and your senses live—that is what hell is. Where your mind lives *here*, is what hell is. And it is that same place that becomes hell *there*.

Besides the spectacle that the eyes can show you, they have another Power within. There is a Light within the eyes. What the external eyes see are the scenes. What is looked at is what is seen. But within, there is a Light. If you examine and discriminate and look with that Light, then you will understand the difference between good and evil, right and wrong. If you discard the external vision and look within, if you look within, then you will know the Truth of the creation of God.

There are these ears which enjoy all of the various sounds and musics of this world. But within, there is a Microphone which is capable of receiving the Sound which emanates from God. It is able to receive the sounds that come from the heavens, from fairies, from angels and other Divine beings. It is possible to receive these sounds with the aerial of Wisdom, and if you examine and begin to appreciate that Music, then His Speech, His Word, and His Explanation will be continuously received by you. You can hear that beautiful Divine Music.

There is the nose which is constantly smelling and taking in the fragrance of everything. It tries to examine the various smells and utilize them for itself. It says, "I like this smell; I do not like that smell..." This ability of the nose to smell is similar to the dog's. If there is an object upon which the blood of an animal or a man is smeared, then the dog can identify that scent and trace it back to its source. There is a piece of flesh at the tip of the dog's nose with which it can do this. Whatever has been touched or used by another, the dog can identify it and recognize the scent. But besides this kind of ability, there is another capacity to detect scents here in the *Arsch* [at the top of the head], a capacity to smell that is known as Divine Luminous Wisdom. If you begin to inhale that Fragrance through that capacity of smelling called Divine Luminous Wisdom, then all of the Fragrances of God and His Qualities will come there. You will be able to lose yourself in ecstasy in that experience.

Man has a mouth. When you came here, you did not have teeth. During the period of a year, the teeth began to come. They erupted very quickly, and once you had them you were able to grind and masticate and taste all of the things of the world. And these teeth smile at the world in so many ways. In 36 different ways you show your teeth to the world. Very soon, the teeth also fall out. Then there is this tongue which babbles. It says good things and bad things, things that make sense and things that do not make sense. It speaks evil things and vulgar things. It says all things.

But we have to think about this. Among the creations of God, man is indeed the most high, the noblest. There exists what is called Man-God, God-Man. God did not create anything greater than man. He is indeed the noblest of God's creations. Yet at the same time it is also true that there is no more dangerous animal than man among God's creations. He can become Satan. We do not have to be afraid of any other Satan, for if man becomes satanic, it is a total danger. If man becomes a beast, he does not let any being alone; it is not possible to escape from him. He will devour every one. And if man transforms into Satan, he would destroy the entire earth.

But if man transforms into God, then with His Love and Compassion he will embrace all beings. So, if these satanic and beastly capacities and the propensities of the teeth and of the tongue can be controlled, and if, with Wisdom, he can extract the taste and the pleasure of the Divine within him—if this transformation can take place—if he can take in that Divine Taste, then he would have become God.

LEX HIXON

Guru Bawa, I have a couple of points that I

want very much for you to weave into a discourse if you would. The first is the question of the Guru's Grace. What is it, and how does it actually operate?

GURU BAWA

First, about Grace...

LEX HIXON

...The Guru's Grace...

GURU BAWA

It is possible for the child to ask about Grace, but how can it be understood? In the earth, there are 4 quadrillion kinds of colors. There is petroleum in the earth. There is iron in the earth. There are various kinds of gems and diamonds. There are so many things in the earth—gas, oil, mercury—all these different kinds of elements are within the earth. One must be able to recognize what it is that a person needs. There are some who need lead, and there are others who need iron. There are those who need gold, and others who need jewels and diamonds. Like this, my brother, to be able to recognize what each person needs, there must be Grace.

It is not magic. It is not a mantra. It is not a religion. It is not a color. It is not anything that has an equal to It. It is not a moon or a star or a sun. It is a Power. So, it is only one who knows about all of the different things that are in the earth who can provide everyone with what he needs.

Suppose you look for a precious stone. Even after you find the stone, you have to discover at what point within that stone its brilliance exists. You must know within the thickness of a thread just where to cut it, and you must know exactly how to facet the diamond to give it its proper shape. You have to know all of these things. It is only at this point that one can give a value to that stone. Until one can do this, there is a need to learn, to study, and to be trained. There is a need to search for and stay near someone who knows about these things, to find someone who knows this section thoroughly and learn from him.

Studying that within yourself, understanding that, digging and finding and then cutting and then finally seeing the Power that is within—that is what is called Grace.

Everything about a man can be measured except for the heart of man. That cannot be measured. You must go on separating and examining and cutting, cutting, cutting each of the things that are within you with Wisdom. You have to examine the earth. You have to examine the fire. You have to distill and discover the things that are in water, and separate and understand the powers of the air, and examine and understand and cut the powers of the ether and the various colors. If one goes on cutting away all of these things and discarding them in this way, he comes to That which cannot be cut, That which cannot be discarded, That Thing which is of God—Grace. That which cannot be overcome or cut by Wisdom, which cannot be cut any more with the thing that you have, That is God, That is Grace. That is what Grace is. Before that, if you are told, you will not understand. Before that [realization], magic can be shown to you, but the Truth cannot be told to you. The moon can be shown to you. The stars can be shown. But This cannot be shown. Therefore, one who has learned the Truth will not show anything. You have to go to that point, and then everything will be shown to you. This is the way the Truth is.

What was the next question?

LEX HIXON

What is the difference of approach between the mind and the heart?

GURU BAWA

There is a thing called love. For example, take a cow or a bird; whatever it may be, it has love, the capacity to love. Animals have this capacity. Even Satan has this capacity. There is love in all of these things. A snake loves its babies very much, but it bites someone else. The lion is very much in love with its children, but if something else approaches, it will kill and eat it. The tiger is the same way. Is this what love is?

No, it is not this. There is the Love of God,

or Divine Love. That Love—that Divine Compassion—is the recognition of all beings as one's own being, as one's own self. That is God's Duty. With that Love, with that Compassion, God can be reached. That is His Work.

LEX HIXON
Sometimes it seems as if the mind is an analytic tool and the heart is an intuitive one. Does Guru Bawa see any difference between them?

GURU BAWA
Outside and inside are there. Whatever we see that makes us happy, that makes us laugh, that gives us pleasure and joy, whatever we love, all of these come from the monkey mind. But there is another point where, "Nothing, I am not", is said. Both are there. Both the one who is a drunkard and one who is Divinely Wise are there, and both are right. One has taken opium, brandy, marijuana, all of these intoxicants. He is completely drunk and intoxicated. In his state of intoxication, he thinks that the road is going up and down, or that the houses are coming towards him. He does not consider the fact that he is the one who is moving and that all of the other things are stationary. When he is walking on the road and someone else comes by, the other person must try to avoid him because this man is swaying this way and that. If the drunkard bumps into him, he blames the other man, saying,

"Why are you hitting me? Don't you know the road? What is this?" And in his state of torpor, he will go and fall somewhere and sleep.

Then a thief will come by, thinking, "That fellow may have some money in his pocket!" And he will take the money and go away. Another fellow will come and take his coat and go, and another will take his shirt. Finally he will not even have anything left to cover his backside. But *he* thinks that he is at home sleeping, and he is quite comfortable. He thinks that where he has fallen is his home, his palace, and his bed. He thinks he is home with his wife and children. He does not know anything.

Now a *gnani,* a Divinely wise person, is also like this. He also has nothing. He has a loin cloth. The world is not near him. He sits by a tree and stays. He stays looking toward God. It could be said that they are both in the same place, or the same state. Neither sees the world. The drunk does not see the world, and the *gnani* does not see the world either. Is this drunkard therefore a *gnani?* Does he have wisdom? Has he reached God? No, he is in an unconscious state where he does not know anything! There is a difference between the two states!

The *gnani* has discarded everything and, without the faltering of his Wisdom, he has proceeded in the straight path to God. The other one has destroyed his entire wisdom and, in a fallen state of wisdom, has lost everything.

The drunkard, in 12 to 24 hours' time, comes back to consciousness and realizes what has happened, that he has lost everything, and goes to his house. But the *gnani* rises and sees that the world is finished. He rises and proceeds to God. This is the difference. There is a similar difference between going with the mind and going with the Truth and Wisdom. This is the difference.

In the operation of the senses, there are five types of consciousness or wisdom. They are the wisdom or consciousness of the earth, the wisdom of the fire, the water, the air, and the ether. These five "wisdoms" or states of consciousness are within all beings, even cattle. These five are within all. But for man, the human being, there is another state of wisdom: *Pahutharivu*, or Divine Wisdom, which is able to separate, to discriminate, and to examine. It is like the sieve used in the panning of gold, with which you pan out all of the dross and take the gold alone. This section of *Pahutharivu*, or Analytic Wisdom, is that capacity with which you strain out the aspects of earth, fire, water, air, and ether, and keep only the section of Man-God, God-Man—that Power. It separates that out. When it is strained like this, that which is of value goes to the section of God, and that which is of the earth is

27

discarded. In the section of the earth, there are countless glitters! But for man, besides the (outer) five wisdoms or states of consciousness, there are an inner seven states of consciousness.

When something comes and scratches you on your body or your leg—like the sensation that we feel when a mosquito or a fly comes and bites us—immediately we hit it. Reflexively we hit it. We think, "What is this that came and bit me?" and we examine and see what it was. "Was it a fly? Why did it bite me? What is it? Is it an ant? Is it a fly?" So, if we examine that process we see that first we feel something. That is *unarchi,* feeling. Then we become aware of it. That is *unarvu,* awareness. Then there is *pudthi,* or intellect—that which tells you what the biting object is. It says, "Oh, this is a poisonous thing!" and you slap and kill it.

Like this, when the mind is crawling along, when these five elements are crawling along and they are biting, see it with Wisdom and say, "Oh, what is this?" and smash it!

The monkey mind travels all over the world and brings back all kinds of things. It looks at all of these things and brings them all back to you, and then you feel it crawling inside of you, within your chest. As you become aware of this mind, you must say, "Oh, what is this thing?" When you recognize that they are the things that the mind has brought, knock

28

them off, push them away! With your *pudthi*, your intellect, your intelligence, knock them away.

With a fourth state of wisdom, we have to think, "This mind is bringing all kinds of things. It is building houses for me to live in. What is this earth, fire, water, air, and ether? Look at this [body]—what is this thing? Who am I? What kind of house should I live in? Where am I going? What is this thing?" This is called *mad-thi,* or judgment, estimating yourself. "Where am I now, and where were we before [birth]? And what is this house [body], and whose house is it? What is it? Is it a rented place? Is it a cooperative store? Is it a store? Is it a stage? Is it a music auditorium? There are all kinds of things happening here: people come; some dance; others sing; they come and go. What is this? There are all forms of activity going on in here. There is one who comes like a ghost; another comes like a lion; another like a demon. There are all these entrances and exits. It is like a big jungle. They have all come here inside me, and they are performing their acts. They sing and dance, they come and go and grab. There is a lot of very dangerous activity going on. I came here to learn. I came here to learn my lessons. I am paying my rent, but there are all of these other forces and people who have come in here. What is this? They are not letting me continue my studies. They are not letting me examine things. They are not allowing me to take my examination. The dog is on one side, shouting, 'Aowooo!' The fox is on the other side, howling, 'Aowooo!' The demons are on another side, shouting, "Aaaaaaah!" Their teeth are showing, and they do not let me do anything. There is this work that I have come here to do. What is this? Whose house is this?"

So, I have to examine this house that I live in now and find what it is and of what substance it has been made. I must discover how it is built and in what design it has been made. And having understood all of these things, I must think, "I must build a house that is beyond all of these things, one that will not be eaten by the earth, that cannot be destroyed by fire, that will not be washed away by water or blown away by wind, a house that is beyond any kind of decoration that colors can give to it. It is that kind of house that I must build, for if I do not have a house like that, then I cannot exist. I cannot exist in this crowd. The sections in this present house are warring with each other. Water is against fire, the earth is against water. Wind is against water, the colors are against something else. This is no good. If I continue to stay in this place where one is fighting with another, it will be a very big trouble for me. I cannot stay in this area."

LEX HIXON
Guru Bawa, about the five elements: If

God alone exists, then He must have also projected these five elements. And if there cannot be anything else but Him...

GURU BAWA

That is true and very important. Everything is His creation.

The Soul is His Light, a Power. It is from There. It is something that cannot be consumed by fire or by anything else. It is His Power. It is indestructable; It is everlasting.

But this earth and all of the other things are creations and are subject to change and transformation. If you take a stone and throw it into the air, will it keep on going up? No. As far distant as the power of the moon, everything that goes up has to come back down because of the power and pull of the earth. It pulls things back to it, here.

But, *that* Power is pulling There. It has no shadow. God has no shadow—no form and no shadow. These other things, however, have shadow. If you light a lamp, that has a shadow. If you look at an ant, it has a shadow. Whatever is made by science has a shadow, also. All of these things that have shadows are subject to transformation, to change. They come and they go. They are in one form and they change to another form.

LEX HIXON

In your consciousness of God there is no

shadow... Perhaps there are no shadows. Perhaps shadows are illusory.

GURU BAWA

Whatever has shadow is destructible. It will be destroyed. Everything that has a shadow will be destroyed; it will die, it will change, and it will come in different forms. This is now called the City of New York. Once upon a time it was under water. This was ocean. Some other time it may have been a mountain. At some point, this area may have been full of forests and jungles. But now it is a city with the name of New York. This is something that changes. *That* is an unchanging Thing.

LEX HIXON

When one is conscious of this unchanging Thing, can you still see the changes?

GURU BAWA

Before That can be known, before the Unchangeable can be known, the changing thing has to be understood. Without knowing this, That cannot be known.

LEX HIXON

But assuming that one knows It, as in the case of Guru Bawa, can he see the changing and the unchanging simultaneously?

GURU BAWA
[interjects]

I do not know! I do not know! I am still learning. I have a lot of work to do, I am studying...

LEX HIXON

Guru Bawa, will you sing us a song, for our meditation and so that the people who are listening will be able to meditate and people who are here will be able to meditate?

GURU BAWA

O Treasure unknown to the chest,
  O Treasure unknown to the chest,
O Formless Form,
  O Treasure unknown to the chest,
O Formless Form,
  O rare Treasure,
May You come and comfort the mind.

O rare Treasure,
May You come and comfort the mind
  So that the Heart may open;
So that the Heart may open
  and so that beings may live;
So that the Heart may open
  and beings may live in Completion.
So that the five may transform
  and be clear,

So that Your Grace may come and shower,
  so that Your Grace may come and shower,
Welcome, welcome.
  You are welcome,
O God, my Father, You are welcome here.

May You come.
May You be absorbed within lives,
And may You Grace their Hearts
  by opening them;
May You Grace their Hearts
  by opening them.
You are welcome my God.
You are welcome
  my God, my God, my God.

May You exist within the reflection
And provide that Grace of the Word
  through which You perform.
May You exist within Clarity
  with Love.
May You provide the Grace
  and the Meaning and the Bliss.
May Your Grace come here,
  may Your Grace come here,
  may Your Grace come here,
May Your Grace come,
  may Your Grace come,
  may Your Grace come,
May You come, may You come,
  may You come.

O my God, O God,
O my Lord who is my Father,
  O my Lord, my Father,
O the expanded Effulgence,
  O God who is resplendent,
O the One who resonates within Grace,
  O the One who resplends,
O the One who resonates,
  O the One who shines all-knowing,
You are welcome, You are welcome,
You are welcome.

May You provide the Word
So that there may be Clarity
  in the reflection.
May You provide the Grace
  so that the self may melt.
May You provide the Grace,
  the Blessing that will last forever.
O my Lord, O my God,
  O my God, O my God,
O the Great One
  who became the Effulgence,
O Lord who became
  the Omnipresent Resplendence,
O the Great One who mingles
  within life and food,
O God, my Father, may Your Grace come.

May You live within the chest
  and change the thoughts.

And may You provide as Love and Grace
   in the self within, my God.
O Celebrated Jewel,
O Lord who is the Complete Life
   in all of the concealed lives,
O the One who is alone,
   Who does not create anything else
   like Himself, O my God,
May Your Grace come.
May You pardon all mistakes,
   O my Father,
And may You arrive.
May You exist within all lives
   and help them all
O my Father, O God, O God.

O the singular Thing
   that knows the self,
You are the Grace
   that provides the comfort.
You are the One
   who bestows Compassion on beings.
You are the Righteous One,
You are the One
   of the Blessed Qualities,
You are the One of the Beauty
   of the Wisdom of the Divine,
May Your Grace come.
May You regard our plight
   and provide Your Grace to beings,
My God, O my God.

May You provide the Grace,
   O my God.
O the One who became the Father,
O the Grace that exists
   within the self,
O the Treasure known as Effulgence
   that became common to everybody,
You are welcome,
You are welcome.
Amin.

LEX HIXON
Guru Bawa, if children came to you, would you accept them as your special children, would you guide them as their own personal father?

GURU BAWA
I am a slave. To the children, I do the work of a slave. I am a servant. The work that has been told to us, we do. And the work that I have learned, I train others to do. And the work that I know of, I teach others about. This is the work of a slave.

LEX HIXON
Thank you, thank you very much.

Truth & Light

WBAI Radio
New York

Sunday morning
October 14, 1973

LEX HIXON

Guru Bawa, we thank you very much for coming again today.

GURU BAWA

God bestows His Compassion upon all beings, always, and His Love and His Way is to bring lives together by pressing them together. God possesses a Love which spreads and intermingles with all lives. In the same way, among human beings there is also such a true Love, such a true, real feeling. When that Love is operating, when it is working, then it is God's work to take it and put it in its appropriate place. That is the Form of Love. That Love, that Divine Love, has brought us together as one.

May God bestow His Compassion upon us, so that that Love will always bring us together and keep us together. May He provide us with that Love and that Compassion.

LEX HIXON

Guru Bawa, there must be some practical path to contacting the Divine Love, to become one with It. The word "meditation" is often used, although there are many meanings to the word. What do you request your students to do in the form of meditation? What are the misconceptions that people hold about meditation?

GURU BAWA

It is a big thing that you have asked about. It is not possible to explain it in a few words. Later, when we talk and give a discourse, we can talk about it in greater detail. For now we will give a short amount, a small point, about it.

Praying, worshipping, and meditation are not ordinary words. When you say "meditation," there is a point in it which is very, very, very subtle, very sharp. First, it must be understood: to whom is the meditation being done? And then, when you say, "meditation," it must be understood: what is meditation? What is it that is called, "meditation?" It has to be understood: who does the meditation? And it has to be understood: for whom must it be done, for whom is it performed? It also has to be understood: why and with what form should we do this meditation?

Now, anything we do without knowing this is not meditation. It is not meditation. Yet, in the world, there are tens of millions of things that are described as meditation. People say they are meditation.

In a body, there are 15 worlds. In this body itself, this section called the body, there are both heaven and hell. There are beasts, there are spirits, there are ghosts, there is hell, and there is heaven in the body. God and man are there, and satan and *maya* (illusion) are also there. All of creation is in the body. All of the manifestations of God have been made into the body of a human.

This is the earth's world. And here, within the chest, is the mind's world; the world of the mind. There is the earth world here, and there is the mind world here. Two worlds are here. And all the things of the earth world exist in the mind world.

Now, if that mind world becomes a place where a *human being* exists, then it becomes a flower world. Then it is called, *"Qalb-pu,"* the Flower Heart. The one who lives in that flower world is God. It is a taste. It is a fragrance. It is a smell. It is that taste, that fragrance, that is known as God.

We have to recognize the point by which that fragrance can be experienced. For that, Wisdom is needed. The Power, the Light of Wisdom are needed to experience the smell. The path of Love is needed, and there must be a park, a flower-garden, where Love, Compassion, and Kindness bloom. In that park, the flowers of Tolerance, of Peacefulness, of Patience, and of Kindness have to bloom, and there has to bloom the Flower of Truth—the truth that there is none other than God and that there is nothing equal to God. It is in *that* Flower that the fragrance exists. So, for that, for the experiencing of that smell, that fragrance, there is no meditation.

If you take in that fragrance more and more, if you catch onto that fragrance, then His Beauty, the Divine Beauty, will increase, and His Qualities will come into it. His Taste is the taste, and His Fragrance is the fragrance, and His Beauty is all beauty. To experience that, Wisdom is needed.

If Wisdom comes, one may know himself. If one knows himself, he may understand who he is. If he knows who he is, it may be known who God is. If it is known who God is, he will know that he is nothing, that this one does not exist. If this one does not exist, then it is God-Man, Man-God. This is the point.

This is not a mantra. It is not a trick or a formula. This is not a religion. It is not something that is within the confines of a race. There is no magic for it, and it is not a yoga. It is not within those things which are described in the four stages of *shariyai, kiriyai, yogam,* and *gnanum* [stages of spiritual development]. This has to be understood.

Only if this is understood, will we understand to whom we are to meditate, who it is that meditates, and who accepts the meditation.

LEX HIXON

Guru Bawa, does one need some sort of technique or mantra to get to this point, or can one just begin at this point of tasting?

GURU BAWA

Yes. If you begin tasting, it will be very good.

If you know yourself, then you can know God. And if you do not know yourself, then you cannot know God.

God has said:

"There is My creation, and I know all of the works in My creation. It is My work to create, to sustain, to nourish, to give judgment, and to raise from the dead. Even for the little atom-like germs that crawl, I am the sustainer, I am the Father.

"For all things—for things that move and for things that do not move, for things that speak and for things that do not speak, for things that glitter and for things that do not glitter—for all of these things—I am the Protector. I have created them. I am the one who provides food for them, and I am the one who summons them. It is My sounds which come through the winds and through the trees and through various things and which may be taken in by various languages as certain specified sounds. I have created all things—and, having distilled everything, having purified everything, having examined everything and taken the best, I have created the human being as My treasury, as My bank, and as My son in such a purified and in such an exalted way. That is what a human being is.

"It is for that human being that I Say, 'I know him, and he knows Me.' If I am to be explained, all of My Wealth has been bestowed upon him. So, he can understand Me, because all of My Wealth is within him. His wealth is Me. His bank is Me. So I am his bank, and he is My Bank. All of My Grace is within him, and all of his things are within Me. This is the way I have created him in a most exalted way.

"If he knows My Beauty, My Qualities, and My Self, then to him I bestow the Kingdom of God. My Kingdom is for him. My Kingdom is for My son. For this exalted action, for this exalted characteristic, the name 'human being' is given. A human being must understand who he is."

There is only one point between these two things. Even atoms worship God. Satan also worships God. Satan may destroy others or mislead others, but he worships God. Illusion worships God and even the earth worships God. There is nothing that does not worship God.

These things have feeling, awareness, and intellect. Even though a being may defecate where it eats and sleep where it defecates, it has the ability and the tuning-in to worship God. It worships through the air, through sound, through breathing. Even the atoms are like that.

But, these things do not have the power of

knowing God, of analyzing things, of separating things and judging, "This is right, this is wrong; this is good, and this is bad." They do not have the power to analyze, separate and understand what a glitter is and what is not a glitter; what a moon is, what a star is, what a sun is, or what a light is. They do not have that kind of discriminatory capacity. They do not have the point by which they can meditate upon God, having understood Him and known what He is, what His shape is, what His form is, and what He is from. The difference is Wisdom, or consciousness.

Now, there are what are known as six kinds of lives. In the human being there are six kinds of lives, and in man there are also six kinds of Wisdom, or six states of consciousness. Now, in these six forms of lives, earth itself (which is one kind of life) has four quadrillion and 10,000 kinds of life forms. It is the mother of the glitters of *maya* (illusion). It is the mother for all creation, for all lights, and for all illusions. It is the mother for all the mantras of the five-letter code—the *pungacharam*. It is the mother of *Om*. It is the mother of all the formulas of *aiyum, kilium, sabum, poium,* [deceitful acts]. It is the mother of that which is known as *"Angena-devi"*—the five kinds. That [earth] alone has so much power.

Fire has 1,008 forms. Whatever you put into it, whether it is good or bad, it will burn.

Water also has 1,008 [forms]. For air, there are another 2,128, and for the ether, for the heavenly forms of the sun, moon, and stars, there are 1,008. So each of these has great amounts of power, or *sakti*. But all of them are within the Power of God. He has with Him the power to control all of these things.

These things are not gods. They are not God. Are they God? Are they Divine? They are things which have been made to be by God. They have been created by God. They have been changed by God, they are being controlled by God, they will be destroyed and then they will be created again by God.

Anything that can be destroyed and then recreated is not God. He who controls them, He who is able to create them, and He who can destroy them, is God.

So you must have that Determination. That is a treasure which already exists within. It is a mysterious thing, and there is no *mantra* for it. You must smell it out. That is the smelling. And that is meditated upon by consciousness, by Wisdom, through your consciousness, through your Wisdom. You must understand: "I am not earth; I am not fire; I am not water; I am not air; I am not ether." Then you must say, "This is all nothing. However far this goes, it has to come back down. The waves of the earth are connected to the earth. This is earth's connection."

But God's connection, the Divine connection, is something which has to be thrown upward. One has to fly with Wisdom and carry that Divine connection. Fly on consciousness and, with that Wisdom, carry it and take it and lodge it within Him. This Divine thing is His. The other is for the world.

So, when you talk about meditation, you must realize this through Wisdom, through analysis. Only after that consciousness has been developed, only after Wisdom has arrived, and only after the analytic power has developed, can we talk about meditation. The rest are just things which go on in the world. This is something we must think about.

What is called meditation is a separate thing. Sacrificing the self is meditation. It is called *"samathi."* *Samathi* is completing the Qualities of God, fulfilling the Qualities and the Contentment of God. So *"Sama-athi"* means the containment of His Qualities. It exists where Completion and the fulfilling of the Compassion of God exists.

For that Truth, the meditation is the sacrificing of the entire self. Meditation is sacrificing oneself and fulfilling the Qualities of God. We will understand what meditation is only if we understand it with our Wisdom.

It is like television. On television we see various things and then discriminate between right and wrong. So, this is something you examine and then perform.

God is not like the sun and the moon. And this is not something like holding our breath. It cannot be worshipped by the air. Nor is it something which can be seen by talking about it. You cannot go to a museum and look at it. It is not something which is heard in music, and it is not something which is seen in acting. It cannot be seen by putting your head on the ground and your feet in the air. Even if we do yoga like a snake, it cannot be seen. That is what snakes do, not human beings. Even if we bend and fly like crows, we will not be able to achieve it.

We must become Human. If we become like a monkey or roar like a lion, that will not be worship. We have to become Human. Man has to become Divine; he has to become God, and what becomes God is His Qualities. That is meditation.

LEX HIXON

Guru, how is it possible for someone to know about this? Before you came to this country, these children here were not looking at the world that way. Therefore, it must have been necessary to come in contact with you.

GURU BAWA

That is possible. But in the earth there are precious stones.

In water there is current. We have always

drunk the water, but it was only after the turbine was discovered and the scientist applied the principle and used the turbine to generate current from the water, that electric current was invented. It was there all the time in the water. It is very difficult to take it, extract it, and bring it outside. Simply drinking the water, or heating the water and drinking warm water, is easy. But it is difficult to make the machines, the engines and the motors, and then take the current from the water to a motor and from there to an engine and from there to the wires and then from there to the various places where it can be used. That is very difficult. To separate that and bring it out is very difficult. But if it is brought, then there is current.

Now, that current must be used carefully. If you put your hand in it, it will give you a shock. It might kill. So it has to be used very carefully. Even if you just touch it, it might kill you. You do not even know whether it is there or not. You cannot see it. Only if you test it with the appropriate instrument—which is what Wisdom is—will you even know whether it is there. So you must use it with caution. It is easy to drink it as water.

Like that, we must extract the Divine Grace. Meditations and things like that are easy; they are like drinking the water. All these meditations, these yogas, these crow-like meditations, these snake-like meditations, the *gnanas* and things like that, are easy things. They are easy. You can drink cold water or warm water, or you can drink it from a stream or from a tap. That is easy. But taking the current out of it, making a motor and bringing the current here, is very difficult. Using it is also difficult; it has to be used carefully, and extracting it must be done carefully.

In the same way, extracting the Divine aspect is very difficult. Bringing it to use is also very difficult. Extracting it and using it is going to be difficult, and you must use it very carefully, or otherwise it will kill. That, itself, will bring about danger.

If we miss our attention—there are four subtle states of attention, called, *"tanum, nidanum, kuvanum,* and *avadanum"* [states of spiritual consciousness]—if that attention is missed even a little bit, then it is dangerous. It will burn. It is a very valuable thing, and not everyone can bring it under control and utilize it. That is difficult. Drinking water is not difficult. Cooking and eating are also not difficult. But extracting is difficult.

Like that, the difficulty is to divide up this body and separate out God and Man from it. That is what is difficult.

LEX HIXON
So, Guru, are you protecting and making

things easy for your children, then? Is that what we are to understand?

GURU BAWA

You say it very easily.

There is rain. The duty of the rain is to rain. And each plant must attempt to get that water for itself.

Now, if you make a pond or a lake, the water will come and stay there. In that water which comes from the heavens there are certain minerals and other things that are useful for the plant. If the water falls on just the earth, then the earth will take it. If it falls on grass, then the grass will take it. If it falls on different plants, then those plants will take it. The skin will absorb certain properties, certain minerals, from the water that comes from the sky. And if the water falls on trees, then the branches, the leaves, and the fruits will draw it in and the tree will become stronger. But if all the water falls on the earth, then the earth will absorb it. It is like that.

So, if there is a lake, the lake will take it; if there are trees, the trees will take it; if there is grass, the grass will take it; or later it might be irrigated to certain crops. The duty of the rain is to rain. The duty of each of these other things is to accept it and take it in. If they do not take it when it is falling, it is not the fault of the rain. The rain will have finished its duty.

So, I cannot carry all these things. I do not have that business. Like the rain which comes down, take it. That is all that can be said. You have to take it, partake of it, grow, and understand and experience that taste. I can teach about the experience. It is experience.

I know about fifty to sixty thousand methods of meditation. I know this. But I did not find them to be of any use. After being unable to get any food, after being thirsty, after experiencing a great amount of pain, and going various places, I finally discovered this way. It is only after I became wise that this path became known.

It is like television now. One is wrong, one is right. One is wrong, one is right. There are only two. There is God, there is the Truth and there are His Qualities. That is right. Everything else is wrong. His Love is right; the love of *maya* (illusion) is wrong. His Selflessness is right; selfishness is wrong.

Now in this life and in that television, all of His Qualities are right. And all the qualities of the earth are wrong. He is right, and everything else is wrong. So, like that, I examine His Actions and His Qualities on that television, and I am able to distinguish between what is right and what is wrong. If you go on subtracting like that, subtracting everything other than Him and His Qualities, then only He and His Qualities, the Truth and His Qualities, will remain. Everything else will go away.

LEX HIXON
Guru Bawa, now we are having this rain rain on us through your words and your Compassion and Wisdom. Is there anything in addition? Is there any "I" of Guru Bawa, or is it simply the Qualities of Compassion and Wisdom?

GURU BAWA
There is a thing called the earth. We give it the name of "earth." But it is possible that there are other things inside it. There is no point in just calling it the earth. It is called the earth, but it is possible there are other things inside it.

As the name "Guru Bawa" is given, the name for the earth is also given. But what is inside is different. The cleverness is in being able to sift out the earth and discover what is inside. In it there are things which go to dogs, to foxes, to worms, and to things like that. That is only one aspect of it. There is no point to that. That is the earth. And there are times when it is necessary to see it and say, "*Aiyo*, poor thing, why did it come here? Why did you come here, poor Guru Bawa; why did you come into this?" There are situations like that.

LEX HIXON
So there are two things, then. You say there is the earth. What is the other thing that is

54

there along with Guru Bawa?

GURU BAWA
That is what we describe as God, Man-God, God-Man.

LEX HIXON
But it is not so clear in the children as it is in the Father.

GURU BAWA
You have to strive. You have to cut it and see what is inside. It is like television; you cannot show everything at once. You have to show a little at a time.

Now, when you tape something new, you have to erase the tape of all the things that were taped before. If you just tape on top of it, it will produce all kinds of noises. You have to erase what is on the tape.

So, my brother, all of the things that have already been taped must first be erased, and then this other message can be written on it.

LEX HIXON
When everything is erased, what is left?

GURU BAWA
If everything is erased, then what remains is what is forever. That is what is recorded there, and that is the eternal. It is the thing that will not be consumed by the earth or fire or by

the air, the thing that cannot be destroyed by earth, fire, air, water, ether, sun, moon, stars, etc. It is the Divine thing, the Divine Quality which is forever, which has no birth and which has no death. That will be put onto that.

LEX HIXON

Guru Bawa, are you able to listen to that eternal tape?

GURU BAWA

That is not something that can be explained by speaking about it. How can I explain that to my brother? If you come, then you yourself can see it.

Now, if you ask whether there is a relationship between the moon, the sun, and the earth, how can that be explained by speaking? Even though the sun may be in the heavens and the moon on the earth, there may be a connection of the rays. It is possible.

That is a different sort of thing, and I do not wish to speak on it.

LEX HIXON

To ask in a different way: suppose if one were to hear that eternal thing, would one then be aware of the world and the multiplicity at the same time?

GURU BAWA

That is God's work.

There is a certain circumstance, my brother. For the Divine Kingdom, the Kingdom of God, there is only God. He is the One who inquires about it and gives Judgements on it. But for a kingdom such as America, there will be different ambassadors for different places. Now, what happens in those separate countries will be told to the American government by that ambassador. According to the law, he will say what has to be said. But he cannot say what is beyond the law.

God is not blind. He is not blind, and since He is able to see everything, since He is listening to and hearing everything, there is no need for us to report to Him. And there is no need for us to think about this. We can just look at it and laugh and smile at it.

If man becomes Human, then he is very large. To him all of the 18,000 universes are very tiny. They are smaller than a particle of a particle of a particle of an atom. If he places his foot in one place, then in this entire universe there will be no room to place his other foot. If he firmly places his foot of Wisdom in this illusory world, then the whole world becomes a tiny particle for him. There is not even a place to put the other foot of Divine Wisdom. The world will be absorbed in him. So why raise up what is under his one foot? It is all under one toe.

It is like that. You might know this later.

Why discuss it? Yes, I can understand certain things.

There is a book that I wrote called, *"Maya Veerum"* (The Strength of Illusion). This is the world. But in the world, to tell the truth is against the law. So can we stay in this world? Can we do that while we are in the world? So let the Truth be with me, and let the world be with the world. If I am to tell the Truth, then it must be brought in a concealed form. To place the Truth there, it must be done as an example through some other thing.

So, like that, I published a book called *"Maya Veerum"*. It was written about 1942. In that book, it has been written all about the various wars that have already taken place and about the war with China, about various things which have come to pass and about the destruction which is to come later. All of these things already have been written about. Like that, certain things have been said. Not directly. It is not said directly. Where some doctor must be mentioned, we might call him a tractor. Instead of "Doctor Thambi," we say Tractor Thambi". That is the way it has to be described; otherwise the law will not allow it. A lot of things have been described in *"Maya Veerum,"* which is written in Tamil.

Sometimes when I know something, I will just say to a person, "This is going to happen to you," and go away. We tell him what is happening, and we go. This is the way it is. But at such a time, it is not what we say. It is like an obsession. We have to say it, so we say it and go. It comes to the mike, the mike brings out the sound at that time, and then it goes away. There is no point in following it through. A certain word came, it was said, and then we go.

This is the way it is. This is the world, my brother. However much learning and understanding there might be, it is not a good thing to say "I" and "mine". It hurts. I am very small. There was a time when I used to do those 50,000 to 60,000 meditations. At that time I used to do those sorts of things. Now [I am] like a little ant, like a little ant. Now I cannot talk like that; now certain explanations cannot be given.

LEX HIXON

Can the children be with you in this state of consciousness? Can your children share this Wisdom that you have gained after so much experience?

GURU BAWA

Yes. Yes, it can be shared.

Aren't you taping it right now? If the tape is right, then it will record. Otherwise it will come back as an echo. Sometimes it is like an echo and comes back. But otherwise, if the tape is right, it will record. .

LEX HIXON

Guru Bawa, some of us feel a longing just to live in God and to regard the world as of no importance whatsoever. Is this possible, or does one still have to be involved in the world?

GURU BAWA

For one who is with God always, it is a lot of work. And for one who is not with God, he has no work. He has work with his house.

God does a lot of work. He has to defend the innocent and protect the rights of those who are supposed to be guilty. And sometimes a rich man might kill somebody and then take a plane to another place in order to find an alibi. He will say, "I was here." Then, God has to go on His Airplane and prove that the man was there stabbing someone.

Like that, God has a lot of work. If one is with God, he has a lot of work. All of His Qualities are work. But if one exists in the state of "I" and "mine," then he has housework to do, *maya* (illusion). He has to eat, he has to defecate, he has to make money; he has to do all of those things. For God, each and every breath is work. If one is to be with God, then each and every breath will be work. And it is work without pay; it is selfless work. It is a selfless job. It is not a business, but it is a job.

LEX HIXON

Is there joy or bliss?

GURU BAWA

Today someone is cooking and putting all kinds of candy, sugar, and honey into a pan. But the pan does not know any of the taste. And the plate also knows nothing. The spoon also knows nothing. It is the one who eats who experiences the taste. Everything was cooked there (in the pan), but the one who eats experiences the taste.

Like that, when one is doing God's work, what taste is there for him? It is like the pot or the pan or the spoon. The taste is for God. The man is an instrument.

LEX HIXON

Can you tell us what Divine Luminous Wisdom is? You speak of Wisdom, Divine Wisdom, and Divine Luminous Wisdom. Can you give us some idea of the differences and the development there?

GURU BAWA

Divine Luminous Wisdom—it is an English word, an English phrase. I do not understand English very well.

It is Truth. It is a vibration. God's Grace, Divine Grace, is a vibration. The power of that vibration is a Light. And the power of that light is Wisdom. That is called *"Pahuth-Arivu"* in Tamil. It analyzes and discriminates between wrong and right. Having analyzed, it takes what is right and discards what is wrong.

Because that Wisdom, that consciousness, comes from that vibration, that Grace, it is called Divine Luminous Wisdom.

LEX HIXON
So this is meditation? There is nothing else to practice?

GURU BAWA
When you say "meditation," if it is without Wisdom, without consciousness, then for whom are you meditating?

The mind can prepare all sorts of things for us. For instance, it imagines a snake as a god, or a crow as a god. For some people a dog is a god, a lion is a god, a cat is a god, a peacock is a god, a crow is a god, a chicken is a god, the moon is a god, the sun is a god, stars are gods, scorpions are gods, cows are gods, donkeys are gods, pigs are gods, and horses are gods. Like this, all these things such as cats, rats, mice, and elephants have become gods which the mind has prepared. Who has prepared them? The mind has prepared these various things. Just what are these gods? If one bomb comes, they will all shatter to pieces. They will all die. When the lion goes, the dog-child will go. When the cat goes, the rats go. When a mongoose goes, the snakes go. How can these things protect us?

Mind and desire, which are unable to see or experience God, have ventured to think that this is what God may be like. The elephant of arrogance, and religion—which exist in the mind—make something into a god and say, "See! This is what God is like." Or, this rat which crawls into various holes also exists in the mind, which makes it into a god and says, "This is what God is like!" There is also a snake which exists within the mind. So the mind says, "Oh, maybe this is what God is like!" and then makes that into a god. This is the way it is. With the five-letter code of *"pungatcharum,"* people manufacture these things. With that (code), they make up these formulas and call them gods. Man makes such a thing and then asks it, "Oh, please give me something." He is the one who has made it, and he is the one who has to carry it from one place to another. He has to repair it and do all sorts of things for it. So how can that provide him with boons or benefits?

Like this, can a manufactured god provide you with what you need? A person has to do all sorts of things for it. He has to carry it, and he has to bring offerings to it and do all sorts of things for it. How can it help him or provide for him?

We have to understand. We must understand. God is that which is not seen by mind or desire. If one produces a god, then it is produced from the qualities that exist within. If he brings out a *patarakalai* (an image of a god), then he has produced the form that was within his mind. The forms and shapes which are inside are those which he brings outside. And it is the qualities that are within that he brings out. And that is what he meditates upon. But God is not like this.

You can understand what God is like only by understanding through Wisdom. Only then can He be meditated upon. Then He can be meditated upon, He can be worshipped, and He can be praised. But as long as God is not known, and as long as the self is not known, what is there to meditation? What are we to worship? What is the thing that worships? We have to think about this.

When you say, "worship," you must understand what it is and then worship. Only when you know what it is can you call it worship. All the things that are done before cannot be called meditation. Only after that Light comes can the explanation of worship be given. That is television. It is something that is shown when one's Wisdom has come. Then you show it and say, "My brother, this is the Father, this is the Mother. This is the Father, this is the Mother, this is the Sister, this is the Daughter." This can be shown. Then you say, "Good morning," and you greet and hold onto it. It does not take a long time afterwards. But first we have to understand who we are and who our Father is. That is what worship and meditation are.

This is the Truth. This is real. This is something that you directly see, that you directly communicate with. It is something that you embrace and love. This is the way. The Truth is like this. If that consciousness arises, if Wisdom comes, you may see your Father and talk to Him. That Vibration will come and you can see this world with the entire 18,000 universes within it. You can see what is in the ocean, you can see what is in heaven, you can see what is in hell, and you can see Satan. You can see outside, you can see inside, and on all sides it will become clear. You can talk, and you can communicate. That is the Truth. That is the television. It is something you directly see.

For that you need Wisdom. For that you need the Divine Qualities. You need Forbearance and Tolerance and Faith. It is God's Qualities that are described as God. If those Qualities emerge in us, if Wisdom emerges in us, then when you apply the Divine Quality and turn the knob of the television, you will see. The entire universes, everything, may be seen. You can talk with everyone. You can make the earth to rise up and talk with you. You can command *maya* to come, and you can ask her, "What are you doing?" You can call Satan and say, "What is this? What are you doing? You do not seem to have any light. What is the matter?" You can talk to him. You can call the sun and ask, "What are you like?" You can call the moon and ask, "What are you?" You can directly talk to things. They will take form and tell you, "This is what we do. This is what we are." You can do this.

This is what Divine Wisdom is, my brother. And this is what the Truth is. This is the Divine Power. And this is the work of the Prince of God. Not the other section. You have to turn it upside down and see it like that.

It is difficult, but we have to turn our life the other way around. That is the meaning, and that is the way the Truth is. This is my personal experience.

LEX HIXON

Guru Bawa, would God do some work in the form of a song?

GURU BAWA

God can sing from you, my brother.

Who are we to finish singing about Him? We can not do that. What worships God is God Himself; what praises God is God Himself; who knows God is God Himself; who meditates upon God is God Himself. Talking about God must also be done by God, and the one who does God's work also has to be God.

So if God is to be sung upon, then it is God who has to sing it. All of His work is something He has to complete. How can we do it? If we try to do it, it is wrong; there will be wrong there. So we must say, "We do not want God's work. You must do Your work Yourself. Then all the faults and credits from it will be of You. It is not something of me."

We have to give each one of our breaths into His responsibility, and then we can escape. Only then can we see.

SONG

O God, may You come
So the Heart will get soft,
And provide us with Grace.
So that Love may ooze forth,
So that Your Grace may shower upon us,
You have to come upon us, O God.

O the One God
Who is able to know all thoughts,
Unlike the lesser gods,
The devas and the munivers,
And Who provides us with His Grace,
O God, You must come upon us.

O my God, O my God,
May You come upon
My dear fellow brethren
So that Your Grace may resonate
Within their hearts,
So that Your Grace may resonate
Within their hearts.

Who is it that can praise You, O God?
Who is it that can sing Your praises, O God?

O the Able One
O the One Who is everywhere,
O the Great One,
It is You Who has to come, O God.
May You come upon us.

O God, the self has to open.
O God, You have to come and reside there
And make it become golden,
So that the Heart will be oozing
Forth with Your Grace,
So that it will come billowing
Forth in Your waves
Of Your Grace.

O God, may You come
To pardon us for the sins
That we have committed
Knowingly and unknowingly.
O my Father, O my dear Father,
O my God,
May You come upon us to pardon us.

O God, the Heart has to open.
O God, the Light of the Gnostic Eye
Has to shine.
The Gnostic Eye has to open
And the Light has to shine.
O God, Your Love has to resonate
In the hearts,
O God, You have to come.

All lives have to be treated
As one's own life.
All lives have to be treated
As the lives of this earth
Which are the same.
O God, O God who is silent,
And who resides in the beautiful
Palace of Silence,
May You come upon us
So that Compassion
Will spread everywhere.

O God, Who exists everywhere,
Who knows every breath and every speech,
Who exists within every breath
And every speech,
You have to come
Because there is nothing of which
You do not know,
Because there is nothing
You are unaware of.

O the Great One who resides
Where the mind cannot see,
O the Great One who exists
Where desire cannot feel,
O the One who exists, O the One,
You have to come within the hearts
And protect us all within Your Love.

Even if millions and millions
Of acts of piety

Are performed in Your Name,
If Your Qualities, if Your Forbearance,
And if Your Patience do not come,
Is it not true that Your Grace
Does not ever come?

O God, may You come perfectly
Upon the straight path
To open us out.
May You come in the speech,
In the thought,
In the hearing,
In the smelling,
And in the meaning.
In all of these things
May You come and be with us,
O God.

O God, my Protector,
What is needed within the eye is
Your Vision.
We need the Grace by which we see nothing
Other than You.

In our ears we must hear Your sounds.
All other sounds must be closed out,
And we must hear
The Sound of Your Grace.
And cease to hear
The sounds of ignorance.

O my God, my God,
Within the nose we need Your Fragrance.

Within the nose we need Your Fragrance.
We have to experience Your Fragrance,
Your Qualities,
And obey You, and be obedient to You,
And follow You until we reach You
And embrace You.

O God, may You reside within our tongues
So that our speech,
Our words,
And our sounds are Yours,
So that we may speak Your words
Amongst our friends and relatives
And increase Your Grace thereby.
O my God, You have to come amongst us
And reside within our tongues.

As Wisdom within wisdom,
As Love within love,
As the Tongue within the tongue,
As the Light within the light,
As Compassion,
May you protect us,
Our dear, dear God.
Our dear, dear God,
Fund of Compassion,
The Station of Trust, O Friend,
Our Original Lord
May You Grace us today.

O God, it is Your responsibility
To come amongst us.

O God, O Lord,
The Protector of the Universes,
Ya Rabbil Alameen,
It is Your responsibility
To come amongst us,
Amongst my fellow brethren,
Amongst my fellow beings,
And protect them so that Wisdom
Will come from them,
Will emanate from them,
And Love and Your Compassion
Will spread amongst them.

Ameen.
O Father, O Dastigir,
Please come and protect us
Without letting go.

Ameen. Ameen.
Ya Rabbil Alameen.

LEX HIXON

Guru Bawa, will you be our spiritual friend even when you go back to Ceylon? Will you still be with us?

GURU BAWA

The body is in a certain way, but there is a thing which does not go and does not come. It is forever where it is. That is a thing. It is not in a place; it is *there*.

It is not the mind. The speed of the mind is

even greater than the speed of air. And wherever it goes it will not stay there but will return.

But the Truth alone will not come back. It has a speed which is immeasurable, and it vibrates from wherever it is. Wherever the switch is turned on, it goes there. And the more switches that are put on, the more light there will be.

LEX HIXON

Thank you for putting electricity in our house.

GURU BAWA

God will provide it.

My greetings to everybody. Greetings. May God provide my brother with long years. May He provide him with many years of life, with His Grace, with His Wisdom, and with His Light. May God protect my brother.

May God provide more and more Grace to you and to all who are associated with you. You have the ability to help children like ourselves, to make our hearts happy by bringing about certain situations. May God protect you and sustain you and provide you with more and more Grace and more and more of His Benefits. You are an example of the other Love and the other Wisdom. You are a help to the children; therefore may God protect you.

Truth & Light

KQED Radio
San Francisco

Saturday evening
October 27, 1973

WILL NOFFKE

Namastay...

We offer this program with humility and a compassionate awareness of our own predicament and yours. We are all on the journey towards enlightenment, and at each stage we must share what has been discovered with those who will listen. The sharing is part of the work, the listening is part of the work. We are all on the path. But where do we begin? The answer is simple. You begin just where you are. Then you become aware of the inevitable process of the evolution of consciousness. Then daily, slowly, the cloud of illusion becomes thinner and thinner until at last there is light. These programs represent a wide variety of techniques. Everyone's needs are different, and everyone is at a different stage along the path. Choose what suits you. If you listen to your own inner voice, it will tell you where you are now and which method will work best for you in your evolution towards the light. Our guest this evening is His Holiness Guru Bawa, and I'd like to introduce you to a president of one of the Guru Bawa Fellowships, Mitch Gilbert, who will introduce Bawa.

MITCH GILBERT

It's always difficult to try to introduce Guru Bawa. It's difficult—it's impossible. That

One that is Guru Bawa for me is known only through some kind of experience that occurs within me. I can see the 90-pound frame and the dark face and the happy smile and the deep eyes and the compassionate expression. But the experience is something that each person has to have for himself. And so there is no way to introduce that experience other than to let each person have that experience.

But it might be of some interest to know that when I first heard about Guru Bawa and was invited to go listen to this guru who had come to Philadelphia, he was living in a row house in the western section of the city. After whatever number of experiences I had had in some 20 years of being on and off the path, I just didn't feel that it was likely that I was going to find a true Guru living in a row house in West Philadelphia. Also, at that time, I was convinced that it was pointless to be looking for a Guru at all. I believed that all of the answers we were looking for were recorded somewhere inside of us. Somehow, we had to find the way to break through that illusion of separation between what was outside and what was inside. If we could do that, the answers were there. But I didn't believe there was any way in the world that someone outside yourself could tell you where that Truth was.

So, with that in mind, I told the dear friends that kept asking me to come that I thought we were being guru-groupies, chasing after each guru that came in. And Lord knows, in the last 12 years there've been a lot of gurus in the United States. So I really considered it a pointless endeavor. But they invited me to a nice dinner with them before we went, and there wasn't anything in particular that I wanted to see on television, or any good movie playing, so I went to the dinner and went to see Guru Bawa afterwards.

That first encounter—and this is the reason why I say that it is so impossible to try and say who the Guru is—in that first evening, I discovered that there was something I call a "tuning fork" that vibrated somewhere inside my heart to the points he was making and the sound of his voice and the smile and the obvious love that he shed on everyone who came into his presence. And after all of these years of saying that I had to be in touch with my body, to discover that there was some instrument in there that I never knew was there before—in spite of all the meditations and all the trips and various techniques that we all used at one point or another—that was the first shock.

As time wore on, I began to understand something that Bawa had told all of us. He said that all of these great experiences that we think we've had and that we believe in are frequently like stars that shine in the night. Darkness is necessary in order for those stars to exist, to have any attraction for us. When the sun comes up, the stars are still there, but they have lost their power over us. They have lost their attraction. They have lost their magnetism. Now there is only that light, and the rest ceases to be.

Well, most of us live in the darkness of our own ignorance. So, if I could understand this Luminous Wisdom, this Effulgent Divine Consciousness that Bawa talks about, then the sound that I used to hear in my ear when I was meditating and thought was God, the light that I used to see and thought was God, all such things would fade away. All the psychic light shows—all the magic—and all the glitters of the world would still be around. But, like the stars, they would disappear as the True Light came. And if there is anything else I can say to explain who the Guru is, it is simply, He is the One who brings that Light.

Perhaps you would like to ask Bawa something yourself that would give him an opportunity to answer you and maybe some of the people in the listening audience.

WILL NOFFKE

Thank you, Mitch. Indeed I have seen the luminous light. That is, I have had the opportunity twice now, since Guru Bawa has been in town, to share the glow around him. Guru Bawa, I have heard you speak of Wisdom, and I was wondering if you could explain how Wisdom can be achieved, whether it is through intelligent study, or through meditation, or through esoteric practices. What is the method?

GURU BAWA

There are six kinds of wisdom, six kinds of lives, six kinds of consciousness. There are water-life, earth-life, fire-life, air-life, ether-life, and *Light*-Life. That which is called Light-Life is God. It is a Ray that comes from God. That Ray is the Power of God. It is the Soul. It is without shadow. It is without end. It has no form. That magnet Power is God.

Of these six kinds of lives, it is for the Light-Life, this sixth Life, that God has made that Treasure called "Divine Consciousness" as His Secret—Wisdom.

That Wisdom, that Consciousness, is God's Grace. That Grace is a Mystery. That Mystery is God's Treasure. That Treasure is God. It is the Human Being who has that Light-Life within him. It is man who has been provided with the Wisdom to understand this. If we are to learn this, we must know that these five lower kinds of life will not understand this. Their consciousness operates only up to the extent of intelligence, or intellect. There are feeling, awareness, and intellect—things that are felt, things seen with the eyes, and then the descriptions of those things. That is the extent of intelligence. Even a snake has that feeling, that awareness, and that intellect. The monkey also has the same thing.

The end result of intelligence is philosophy and religion. The highest point, the final point, to which religion and philosophies can reach is the intellect. This is the level of consciousness that exists in animals and all other things. God says that, in all of the many creations, He created all of those things, and He filtered out the most valuable Treasure, His Secret. That Secret is Man. God's Treasure is Man, and Man's Treasure is God. All of the Wealth of God is in Man, and all of the Wealth of Man is in God. The Consciousness which can understand this is called "Wisdom." That Consiousness belongs to Man. That Wisdom exists only in Man. Whoever is endowed with that Light is called "Man." That is far beyond the borders of religions and philosophies. It is beyond the 64 games that are involved in creation. It is beyond the stages of *shariyai*, *kiriyai, yogam* [the first three levels of spiritual development]. It is beyond that which is called *gnanam* [often considered the final step in spiritual growth].

The next level of consciousness is called "Estimate," or "Judgment." Judgment is the level of consciousness beyond intellect. That is the process of estimating: Where were you before? Where have you come to now? What are you doing now? Where are you going to go? What sort of building is this [body]? Is it destructible? Of what has it been made? Is it something that is subject to an agreement? Is it mine or someone else's? Who is the owner and what is the agreement? Am I the earth? Am I the fire? Am I the water? Am I the air? Am I ether?

Analyze it and separate it like this. Separate it and take the Essence from within it. That Essence is the Soul. Take out that Light. That is what came from God. We have to understand what kind of Treasure it is. To understand that, the estimate—and the control of the powers with Wisdom—has to go beyond the separations of races, religions, and scriptures, beyond philosophies and beyond the states of *shariyai, kiriyai,* and *yogam,* beyond these states of development. It is beyond these things. All of these belong to some aspect of the game of life. They are part of the dance of life—the 64 games of sexual pleasure and the things that we do with ourselves in the darkness. All the donkeys and the snakes and the horses do it. When it is projected outside, it becomes a performance. When it is done outside, it becomes the various arts and the knowledge of the arts. The act that we perform inside in the darkness becomes art when it is performed outside.

Wisdom lies beyond these acts.

There are five kinds of consciousness associated with the physical elements of earth, fire, water, air, and ether. These elements are hostile to each other. They are enemies. They claim the arrogance of "I" and "mine". This body is a cooperative store, and these five are the five shareholders. All of the people associated with the games and the arts are within this body. This body is a museum. It is an art museum. It is also like a zoo. It is a house of illusion. It is a cave full of the arrogance of the elephant. This body is a huge store. It is a business. It is a huge factory that performs "shaker-maker" work [like the shaker-maker toy], in which everything can be done. Whatever it is that is needed, it will shake it and then make it for you. Whatever it is that you want, it will shake it and then make it for you. If you want gold, it will shake it and make it for you. If you want a man, it will shake and make it for you. If you want something else, it will shake and make it for you. This body is a huge store, a company. Understand this. Realize that these five elements are hostile enemies, that this body is a cooperative of enemies.

This analysis has to be done with the sixth state of consciousness, Divine or Analytic Consciousness. With this state of consciousness, you must analyze, separate out, and understand: what the qualities of the earth are, what the business of the earth is, what the energy of the earth is, how the earth operates, what the limitations of the earth are, what the earth can do, and what sort of house [body] this is. You have to understand the qualities of the earth in this way. You must analyze and find out with Analytic Consciousness.

Secondly, what is the quality of fire? There is fire inside the body. It burns whatever we take in. It devours everything. The fire exists. What are its qualities? It burns both the good and the evil. It says, "I!" It says, "There is nothing greater than I am." It burns wood and it burns gold. It tries to burn God and His Love. It would burn everything. It does not discriminate between good and evil. It has selfishness and the "I." Fire has 1008 kinds of powers, the energies of 1008 powers. The earth has four quadrillion, ten thousand glitters which are the powers of creation. For fire there are 1008 energies claiming the "I."

In water, there are the bonds of blood. There is the separation of my religion, your religion, my race, your race, my children, your children, my love, your love. Water maintains the bonds of creation out of semen, which does the work for the cemetery. There is the rolling around of the energy of semen which produces for the cemetery.

Then there is the air which can be called "the mind," the monkey mind. It has 2,128

84

kinds of air-energy. Of these, there are 84 airs which produce diseases. The monkey mind jumps and flies around because of these winds of illusion. But the mind flies faster than the speed of the air. It claims to be going to and coming back from the kingdom of God. The mind must be analyzed, the energies of the mind must be analyzed, the actions of the mind must be analyzed. And this analysis must be done with Analytic Consciousness.

Then there is the ether. The sun, the moon and the stars, the seven colors, and all the glitters must be analyzed. The nature of these colors and their significance must be analyzed. Then we will see that all the things that are contained in the ether—that are in space—are connected to things that are contained in the earth. The things that are contained in the **earth** are connected to the ether. If you want to examine a precious stone that you take from the earth, for example, you have to look at it through the light of the sun.

Ether has a connection with the earth, and the earth has a connection with the ether. Although a connection of ether with aspects of the earth exists, this is not what the ether is. Still, all of these things ultimately return to the earth. All of these glitters, all of these lights are connected to the earth. All of them go through change. And whatever comes in changing forms is illusion. Hell is repeated births in transformed ways. Whatever takes different forms at different times is *maya*, or illusion. All these things have a connection with the earth. The sun and the moon and the stars are not God; they are all aspects of the earth and creation.

This analysis has to be done, and that separation has to be recognized. We have to say, "This is nothing. He is not any of these things. This is not what God is." If we analyze with Divine Analytic Consciousness, the meaning will be within the Soul. Where is the Soul kept? It is God's Mystery. It is Man. The switch for the Soul is with God. The Light of the Soul is here [in the body]. When the switch is turned off, then the Light returns to God. The Light goes to Him. It has come here into the darkness to explain and to radiate outward. It has come here so that it may understand the Secret of the Father, and to learn in this university of the world. This analysis must be done with Analytic Consciousness. This is what Man is; he is not any of these other things. To recognize the Soul and to accept It is Divine Wisdom.

It is only if the Soul is known that the Father may be known. There is a relationship, a connection between the two. There is a connection between the Switch and the Light. If this can be known, then the Father can be known. Only after the Father is known can prayer and worship take place. The understanding with which we know our Father and understand Him—and the use of that Consciousness—is the state of Man-God, God-Man. That has to be learned from a Guru who has that Quality and that Consciousness.

How will such a Guru be? In him there will be no mantras. In him there will be no yogas. In him there will be no selfishness. In him there will be no titles. For him there will be no offices. For him there will be no business. For him there will be no selfishness. For him there will be none of these things. For him there will be no question of great honors. He will be like an ant.

But the Quality of God will be in Him. Divine Love will be in Him. Compassion will be in Him. Forbearance will be in Him. Tolerance will be in Him. Peacefulness will be in Him. Conscience will be in Him. Justice will be in Him. Peacefulness will be in Him. God's 3,000 Compassionate Qualities will be in Him. Those Qualities are God. If that "Form" comes to be, if the "Form" of that Divine Quality comes to be, then the Mystery of the Soul will exist there. The Soul that God has given will exist there. That is why He is called God.

God has no form. God has no shape. God has no shadow. God has no race. God has no religion. God has no colors. He has no red, no black, no yellow, no white. He is not the sun, the moon, or the stars. He is not *shariyai, kiriyai,* or *yogam.* He is only His Compassionate Love. It is His Quality of Compassionate Love that is called God. When all of these things have been understood, when all of these things have been understood one by one, when His Qualities have been accepted, then that will be His "Form." His Grace and His Treasure will be within that "Form." His Beauty will come. His Beauty will come. He will say, *"My Son!"* The Father will say, *"O, my Son, the Prince of God! My Kingdom is yours! My Kingdom is yours. I give you My Kingdom."* The understanding of all this is Wisdom.

WILL NOFFKE

It seems to be the function of the Guru to destroy the ego, and then all of this comes.

GURU BAWA

That is true. But when you first talk about a Guru, you must also talk about the disciples. I have written a book in which one part explains the ways in which to recognize the Guru. In one part of that book, *Divine Luminous Wisdom,* there is an analysis of gurus. An explanation about disciples is also given there. The analysis of how many different kinds of disciples there are and the analysis of how many different kinds of gurus there are, are given there. There is also another book, written in Tamil and called *Guru Mani,* where the explanation about the Guru is given. That book has not been translated yet. But the explanation about the Guru is given in it. If you read it, you will understand.

Everything seen is a guru. Everything must be understood. If you have that Consciousness there will be so much to learn. Whatever we see has to be seen from within that Consciousness. With it, we have to analyze and extract the Secret of God that is within it. We must accept God's Secret within that Consciousness, and we must discard Satan's secret. The Secret of God exists in all the creations of God. The Wonder of God, the Mystery of God, exists in everything. When you realize that, when you begin to recognize your Father, you will say, "Ah, my Father!" He has given such exaltedness even to the atom. When we extract that Secret, we will praise our Father. The Secret of our Father exists in all of the universes. But while there is the Secret of our Father, there is also the secret of *maya* (illusion) and of Satan. The secret of Satan is hell. The Secret of our Father is heaven.

All of this was within God at the time of the beginningless beginning. Before the primal beginning, Allah was in darkness and everything was contained within Him. Everything was contained within Him. The Light that is called the *Noor* appeared from within Him at the time when He was alone in His Meditation. Because of His Meditation, because of His Worship, because of His Prayer, the Completeness, the Perfection that is called the *Noor*, emerged from within Him. It is a Light which came from within Him. It came from within His Heart. Then the world of darkness—the darkness of the beginningless beginning—separated from Him and left Him. The darkness saw that Light and was dispelled.

Then the Light said to God, "O God, this is the world. Look at this. Examine this. O God, all the atoms, every single atom is praising You. Look at that, look at this, look here, and look there; everything came from You and is praising You. It is You whom they worship. They have no form, but they are moving. All the movement vibrates. Look at this! It is You whom they describe! All of these things have movement. You were alone in that darkness for such a long time without recognizing and without hearing all the sounds of all the things that move. Look at this!" That *Noor*, which is called the Perfection and the Pure Light, shows this to God and tells Him this.

It comes from God, and it shows this to God. God originates from the beginningless beginning, and darkness also originates from the beginningless beginning. The aspects of

darkness and the aspects of Satan also origi-
nate from the beginningless beginning. They
both come from Him. Because it comes from
Him and separates from Him, it is natural. God
is natural. Illusion is natural. Light is natural.
Night is natural. It all came from Him. He made
what separated from Him into *duniya*, the
world. He discarded it. That is the world. Then
He became Light. All the Qualities of God
came as Light.

It is also like that for all the qualities that
are within us. When that connection with the
Qualities of the Purity of that Wisdom comes
from within us, when that emerges from within
us, when that Light emerges, then this natural
beginningless beginning, this earth, the body,
the earth, the fire, the water—all these natural,
elemental qualities—will separate out and go
to that other side.

Then only God will exist, because those
qualities will be gone. The quality of the earth,
the quality of fire, the quality of air, the quality
of water, the quality of ether and of the sun,
moon, and stars, the colors and all the satanic
things will move away. Then only God will exist. When Wisdom arrives, these things will be
dispelled in that way. This darkness will be
dispelled. This torpor will be dispelled. This
sensuous love will be dispelled. This lust will be
dispelled. This race consciousness will be

dispelled. The differences of "you" and "I" will be dispelled. Only the Qualities of God will remain. The satanic qualities will be dispelled. Once they have been dispelled, then only God will exist. And at that time, He is called God.

He has no wife. He has no child. He has no form. He exists as Light. For Him there is no torpor. For Him there is no comparison. For Him there is no selfishness. For Him there is no hunger. For Him there is no illness. For Him there is no aging. For Him there is no anger. For Him there is no sin. This is the way it is. It is like this. When these evil qualities are dispelled in this way, and when the Purity comes, then that is the Purity, that is the *Noor*, that is *Gnanam*, that is Divine Wisdom, and that is Grace. That is God. This is the way it is.

WILL NOFFKE
I wonder if we might ask our listening audience to ask some questions of Guru Bawa.

GURU BAWA
If they ask wise questions, questions that will increase understanding, then I will answer them.

CALLER
How can we deal with anxieties that we are confronted with in life?

GURU BAWA

When our life—the life that we think is a suffering—is thought about, we must consider the reason for this suffering. It has been seen that God gives everyone what he needs. In the presence of God, whatever it is that we want, we can ask for it. But we could be asking for burdens that we cannot carry. We ask for the earth. We ask for gold. We ask for offices. We ask for titles. We ask for children. We ask for love in our lives. In our lives, we ask for many things like this. Now when we ask for these things, the burdens become too heavy for us. The burdens become too heavy for the mind to carry. When the burden gets too heavy for the mind to carry, then we look at it and we are bewildered and confused. Our mind has the ability to ask for things that will produce unhappiness.

The mind is a monkey. It is a baby. It is constantly asking for everything. What we call the world is a museum. What is called the mind is a baby, and what is called desire is a dog. When this baby looks at all these wonderful things that are here, it cries and cries. The more of this museum you show to the baby, the more it will cry, saying, "I want that. I want that. I want this. I want this." As we go on getting things for it, it also asks for things we cannot get. This is what causes anxiety. This what causes suffering. This is what causes unhappiness. Then there are difficulties in our lives.

But there is a way out. Whatever the mind asks for, whatever it is that the mind, the desire, our life, and our thoughts ask for, this is what we must analyze with our Wisdom. If, when we analyze it with our Wisdom, it proves to be a correct point, then we must accept it. If it is not a correct point, then we must stop it. We must control it with the consciousness of Wisdom. Whatever it is that the mind asks for, it is from there that we have to control it with Wisdom. The mind will say, "I want that." Then you must say, "Stop! You stay there! Later on we will see about it." Then it will say, "I want something else." Then you must say, "Stop! You wait there! I will deal with that later." It will ask for something else. You must say, "Stop! I will give it to you. It is all for you, so wait. This is a wonderful, mysterious place, this world, and we are going to give it to you." Like this, the way to escape from these anxieties is to control them with Wisdom and to go on to God. This is the way to do it.

On the way to God you need a boat. What is called "Life" is a boat. What is called "the world" is an ocean of illusions. It is an ocean of illusions. You have to row across that ocean with Wisdom. You have to push all the anxiety and unhappiness behind with the oars of the boat. As you travel on the ocean of the mind, use the oars of Forbearance and Love and

Compassion to push back all the unhappinesses and anxieties that the mind brings and all the illnesses and distresses that come in life. Push those things back and row yourself forward, take yourself forward.

It is only then that we can cross this ocean of illusion. It is only then that we can overcome unhappiness and anxiety. You have to push back all the unhappinesses and anxieties that come. You have to push them back with the Qualities of God and with the Forbearance of God. You have to surrender yourself to God. He who created you, provides food for you. A scale can only weigh what it can weigh. A scale that is capable of weighing 100 pounds will not weigh 300 pounds. God knows that. He who created you knows your capacity. He has given you what you can carry. It is because of your ignorance that you have taken on things that you cannot carry. It is your desire and your lust that have made you want to carry all of these things. Those are the things your mind has tried to carry. It is not the fault of God. Therefore, put it down. Surrender to Him, and He will look after it. He will give you a load that is appropriate, that can be carried, and that is appropriate to that scale. My brother, it will be good for you to do that.

SECOND CALLER
Is there free choice, or is that an illusion of

the intellectual mind? Is it all destiny or *karma?*

GURU BAWA

For the Human Being, for the Soul, and for God there is no destiny or *karma.* What is called *karma* is an aspect of your body. It is an aspect of your mind. It is an aspect of the earth in you. It is an aspect of your love of gold. It is an aspect of your desire. In this way, *karma* is an aspect of your body, it is an aspect of illusion, Satan and hell. This is what is called *karma.* It is an aspect of the earth. When you consider where you were before, and if you understand who you are, and if you intend to know yourself, and if you understand your Father, and if you understand to whom you were born, then that is a Treasure which will not die. There is no *karma* and no destiny for It. It does not have an end. It cannot be destroyed. It is something that is always limitless, and It is something that is there forever. It is there forever. You have to understand this.

In the *puranas,* the Tamil scriptures, there is a story about this mind, which produces things. The mind was looking for God. In the Tamil *puranas,* they talk about *karumal* and *thirumal.* What is known as *karumal* and *thirumal* is also known as Krishna, and it is also known as the intellect in the mind. It is said that Krishna is described as the one who lies in the ocean of milk. We know there is no ocean of milk out there. The milk that is spoken of is the milk in the breast. It is this mind which is drinking the milk from this breast. Intellect is called "Krishna." He is also called, "Mahavishnu." He is called "the one who steals women." That is because of this love for the breast. That occurs when he thinks of his love for his mother. First he loves his mother as he suckles her. Then he sexually loves that same breast. That is what is called "the ocean of milk."

Then they describe Krishna as sleeping on Athishaydan, the five-headed serpent. Those are all illustrations, examples. For instance, the five heads of this snake represent the earth, fire, water, air, and ether. They are also the five senses. He who lies on these five senses, and he who lies on this ocean of illusion, he who lies in state on this ocean of milk, is Intelligence. It is sleeping on these five senses. This is the meaning of that illustration.

Then it tells of his playing a flute. He plays the flute and looks after the cows. In Arabic, this is known as *Suratul Bakarah*. There are about 300 verses in that *Surat*. Bakarah means cow. That form of the cow represents this body which is plowing this world with semen. This body is called a cow. It is called a cow. This body is the cow that is plowing this world with semen. This cow, which grazes, is also called "the Intellect." That is the *Mahavishnu*. To illustrate this concept, they made various forms. They drew various pictures to explain this point. That is the meaning of this. That is the meaning of these examples which they showed on the outside. It is due to the examination of only what is outside that this whole question about free choice and the investigation of *karma* arises.

It is for this cow that an agreement exists. That is also the cooperative store, the cooperative store of the hostile forces. This is found in the Hindu *puranas*. Explaining this, they talk about what is known as *karumal* and *thirumal*. Desire is called *"karumal."* The mind is called "thirumal." Mind and desire both started searching for God. They said, "They say there is a God. We must look for Him."

The mind said, "I am going to search in the heavens to see where God is."

Desire said, "I am going to search within the depths of the earth." Desire started searching in the direction of sexual pleasures. Sexual pleasure is what is meant by "the depths of the earth." Desire is searching in that cave of sexual pleasures. When desire went into that cave to search for God, it searched throughout all of the 64 games of sexual pleasures. It searched throughout all of these aspects, but God was not there. Only darkness was seen there. Desire found only demons and darkness and hell. That is what it found.

That which is called the mind searched in

the 64 public arts in what it called "the heavens." The various arts, the sciences, philosophy and yoga, *shariyai*, *kiriyai* and *yogam*, dance, music and magic—all of these things are in the realm of the 64 arts. The mind searched for God there. After searching throughout all the heavens, mind still did not see God. God was not in yoga or in music or in any of those things. The mind became tired and said, "I did not see God. I did not see Him in music. I did not see Him in dance. I did not see Him in that yoga or in that devotion or in that *bhakti*. I did not see Him in that mantra."

In that way, the mind got tired and came back. Desire, having tired of all the sexual games, also came back.

Then the mind asked, "Did you see God?"

Desire gave this reply: "I have searched in all the depths of all the earthly worlds, in all of the 64 pleasures. God is not there. I did not see God on that path."

Then desire asked, "How about you? Did you see God where you went?"

The mind replied, "I have examined all of the sciences, all of the arts, all of the magics, all of the devotions, all practices, all *shariyai*, *kiriyai*, and *yogam*; I have examined all of those things. I did not see God in any of those places. I have examined all mantras, all meditations. God is not there."

Then they said, "Oh, then there is no God.

Only the two of us are here." That is when mind and desire are about to start creating. That is sexual love. Mind and desire make love to each other. That making love is the earth, fire, air, water, and ether. This is what the mind and desire are.

They make all of these toys, all of these forms, and all of these images, but not Life. There is no Life. Because there is no Life, and because they have made all of these things, the Life has come from somewhere else. That Life is called the Soul. Then they say, "These things that we make do not move. Life has to come from somewhere else for the motion to exist. So is that where God will be? Then how will that God be?" Then they see snake. They make an image of that snake and they say, "Oh, is God like this?" Then they see a rat, and they make a little god like a rat and say, "O rat, are you the God that sent this Life here?" Then they see an elephant and make an elephant deity and call it *Pulaiyar*. They say, "O God, O Pulaiyar!" They give it various other names such as *Ganesvara, Eesvara,* —names like that. Then they see a dog. They appeal to it and say, "O God, O God, is this the way you are? Are you what is called God, are you God, God, God, are you God?" Then they see a hen and say, "O God, is this the way you are?" Then they see a peacock. Then they make a peacock image. Then they see a lion. Then they start to

100

worship the lion. But they did not see God. Then they see a cow, and make that into a cow god. They see a horse and they make a horse. They see a donkey and make something like a donkey. They see a crow and they make a crow. Then they see a fish and make a fish, and they start to worship it. They see the sun and then they start to worship the sun and they say, "O Suriya-bhagawan!" They see the moon and worship it, and they say, "O Santira-bhagawan!" Then they see the stars and they call that God, and they start to worship the stars, saying, " O Nadtsattira-bhagawan."

Mind and desire made everything they saw into deities, into gods. In the course of their research into "What is God, what is God, what is God, what is God?" they manufactured four quadrillion, ten thousand gods. They make all these things gods, and they worship them. This is the body. The body is the *karma*. What made it is also the *karma*. The karmic connection between these two things is illusion. It is for these two things that *karma* exists, that destiny exists. Their connection is with the earth and with illusion.

This does not apply to the Human Being. The Soul of Man is Light. It has no birth or death. It has come here to know the Secret of God, to study in this university of the world, to pass the exam and to go on. The Son of God has to go back to God. If this is understood, then it is enough. There is no destiny, there is no *karma* for that. Destiny is for these things that are subject to the agreement. If you understand who you are, then you will understand about destiny and about *karma*. Then there will be no karmic bond for you. If you establish a connection with Wisdom, then you will establish a connection with God. If that connection with God comes, then the Qualities of God will come. If God's Qualities come to be within you, then you will exist forever. There will be no limit for you. My child, it is good if you can understand this.

WILL NOFFKE

That is a beautiful answer. We have another call that has been waiting for quite some time.

THIRD CALLER

If none of these *sadhanas* of the desire or the mind bring about this vision of God, what is it that will bring about in me the condition of complete surrender to the Guru which culminates in that vision?

GURU BAWA

You need Faith. You have to see the Qualities of a true Guru, and you need to surrender to him. Those Qualities will be the

Qualities of God. That will exist without any mantras or tricks. It will be the Word of God, and the Word of God will be One. It will be something without business; it is not in business. He will be working, but without a business. He is not in business. That Guru will not be seeking your help. He will give you what he has, and then he will proceed. You have to have complete Faith in the Guru who has acquired the Characteristics of God. You have to receive the Divine Wisdom that he has with Faith, Certitude, and Conviction. It is that Wisdom, that Consciousness, which dispels the darkness of torpor. If that darkness is dispelled, you will see your original form. If you see that original form, you will know your Father. If you come to know your Father, then there will be no unhappiness for you. There will be Divine Light. That is what the true Guru will give. Understand this.

WILL NOFFKE
There are two questions here that have come in which are quite similar.

FOURTH CALLER
Do you give initiation or experience of the Divine Knowledge so that your disciples can carry on when the Guru is not present?

FIFTH CALLER
Many masters give experience of inner

light or sound as first-hand contact with the word or the nectar of life, or they give some experience of the opening of *chakras*. Why don't you feel the need to give this first-hand experience?

GURU BAWA

Yes, such teaching exists. I will tell you about it. The things that you have talked about and the things that you have done are what I have also experienced. I have learned mantras. I have performed tricks. I have also learned boxing and wrestling. I have learned how to perform many kinds of miracles. I have learned various ways of being a swami and manufacturing deities. I have done a lot of magic. I have made things out of nothing. I have done various tricks, and I have performed various miracles. Long ago I performed miracles. I have also stolen things. I stole some oranges at one time. I stole orange fruit. One day I was hungry and I stole some bread. I also pinched people. I used to do all these things long ago. I have done a lot of little naughty things. I learned yoga. I learned various things about sciences and various medicines and herbs and healing. I trained people to be healers and to be exorcists of witches and demons and so forth. I learned a lot of things like this. I have been in the forests. I have been with and known the hunters of the forests. I have been with and known cannibals. I have done all these things.

What did I do all of these things for? I did all of these things in order to discover God. Yet all of that searching—all of those years—did not lead me to God. It is possible that I had many gurus in respect to all of these matters. The gurus that I have encountered in the jungles in which I have travelled have been very many. I know gurus very well. I can tell fortunes very well. I know the abilities of the mind. I know about hypnotizing. I know a little bit about everything. But none of these things were of any use. I did not see God.

I did 64 kinds of yogas that were associated with the 64 games. I was a guru for the people of each of the four religions for awhile. At one time I was a Bishop. At another time, in another religion, I was a great swami. People gave me all these titles such as swami and all the others, but not for the sake of Divine Wisdom. In Islam, they gave me the title of a great wise person. They gave many things like this to me. But they did not give them to me because of Divine Wisdom. They gave me these titles and other things because of the acts and the performances and miracles. I stayed in the mosque like this, and I prayed and prayed and prayed and prayed. I did all of these things. But I did not see God. I did not see God. God was not there. When I was like that, when I was crying and in despair, when I was in this state, I had to just sit. It was then that my Guru came looking for me. That Guru is the most rare Guru. He came to me and gave me this discourse [He sings]:

He is the Ray resplending from the Sun,
He is the Ray resplending from the Sun
In all of the created beings, each one.
All of them receive His Grace
Through His quality of Grace.
Coming as the Guru of God
To all Lights on earth,
O Father, becoming Good Qualities
By fasting for 12 years.

That Guru is known as Muhaiyuddeen. He came to me. This is the meaning: He is the Sun to all the suns, the Sun to all the Rays, the Sun to all of the Lights and to all of the suns. He is that Original Radiance with that Original Power, with that Original Ray. That is what is called the Power that is greater than power, the Rahumath (Compassion) of God on the Path without equal. This Power provides all of the power to this sun, this moon, and all of these things.

He is the Ray resplending from the Sun,
In all of the created beings, each one.

106

That Power is in all lives, exists in all lives as the "Form" of Love, Perfect in all creations.

He is the Ray resplending from the Sun,
In all of the created beings, each one.
All of them receive His Grace
Through His Quality of Grace.

All of creation receiving the Grace of God Who is the One through the Grace of God.

Coming as the Guru of God
To all Lights on earth.
To all Lights on earth.

He is on this earth for all of the Saints, for all of the Wise men of this earth, for all of the truly Divine Wise men of this world, for all of the Lights of this earth, and for everybody and everything.

Coming as the Guru of God.
O Father, becoming Good Qualities
By fasting for 12 years.

He came as the Guru. He is the Guru for all of the Divinely Wise of this earth. The King of the Gurus was in a state of fasting for 12 years, the fasting being good conduct, Good Qualities. [The fasting of good conduct will be]:

Fasting for a year by cutting off the power of [attention to] the lower excretory opening.

Fasting for the second year by cutting off the power and the pull of the lower opening of creation.

Fasting for the third year by cutting off the evil and poisonous qualities of [inherited through] the navel.

Fasting for the fourth year by cutting off the happiness—the tastes, and smiles, and worldly pleasures—experienced by the opening of the mouth.

Fasting for the fifth and sixth years by cutting off the connection to the fragrances of the earth, to worldly smells and the attachment to these qualities that are inhaled through the nostrils.

Fasting for the seventh and eighth years by cutting off the powers of the sun and the moon which are in the eyes, which are in the openings of the eyes. The sun is in the right eye, the moon is in the left. So there is fasting for two years by cutting off the pull of the gaze of the eyes.

Fasting for the ninth and tenth years by cutting off the power of the ears, which receive and experience both illusory and mysterious sounds.

Cut off the ten sins in this way.

Fasting for the eleventh year by opening the Eye of Wisdom [the third eye], the *Kurusi,* the Eye of Divine Consciousness, God's Light.

Fasting for the twelfth year by seeing the station of the Father in the *Arsch* [the apex of the head]. The Omnipresence of God in His Throne is there.

Having fasted for 12 years like that, having understood these 12 explanations, my Guru is the Guru who explains those things. That is my Guru. He came and He gave me that Grace. It is not with these (worldly) aspects that you can see Him. It is not with these (worldly) aspects that the Grace can be given.

The Word is One Word. There is a Word that He gave. *"La ilaha il Allahoo.* There is nothing other than You. You are Allah." He is the One who exists. There is nothing else. I am not. There is nothing that is equal to Him.

"La ilaha," there is nothing other than You.

"Il Allahoo," You are Allah.

The surrender is saying, "You are Allah." How does that have to be done? With the breath going out and with the Soul operating, that movement of *"La ilaha"* has to start from the toe, and move through all of the 4,448 nerves in the body. That movement has to take place in the blood, in the seven kinds of tissues, in the seven layers of flesh, and in the seven layers of skin. That movement has to be felt in every hair follicle, and in every pore of the body. The movement of that sound has to be felt in the same way you might feel an ant crawling on your body. You have to feel it and be aware of it in the same way. You have to know that word in that way.

That feeling has to come up to the *Arsch* from the toe, and then descend through the left nostril. Feeling has to know that. *"La ilaha,"* there is nothing other than You. That is the way the exhalation has to be done.

This point of Divine Consciousness is God, to whom you have surrendered. As God, He is the only One who exists. He is omnipresent everywhere. Your Consciousness or Wisdom has to stay at that point. You have to draw the breath in as *"Il Allahoo."* It has to stay within your *Qalb,* your heart. There is a church in the *Qalb.* It is known as a lotus flower, or *Qalb-poo,* flower of the heart. In that is the Flower of God Consciousness, the Rose. In that there is a mosque, a church. In that there are indescribable heavenly angels, heavenly messengers, heavenly prophets—Divine Prophets, Messengers. It is not a building made of earth. It is not a building made of fire. It is not a building made of water. It is not a building made of air. It is not a building made of colors. It is not a building made of any of these things.

It is He, it is God's Grace which has built that building. That is the Church. He is there. His Kingdom is there. His Messengers are there. His Lights and His Saints are there. His angels, Gabriel, Michael, Israel, Israfeel, Munkir, Nakir, and all the angels are there. The Day of Judgment, the Day of Life, those who examine those things and those who examine all the records are there. We have to take this Word to that place. *"Il Allahoo,* You are Allah!" That Word has to be recited in that Church. This is what He gave me.

After that, this Word has to be recited with each breath. In one day, there are 43,242 breaths. There are 21,621 breaths taken in. There are 21,621 breaths going out. If you surrender these 43,242 breaths to Him, then that is Prayer. This is my Prayer. If you become like that, the 18,000 universes will all be like a particle within a particle within a particle within a particle. You will be able to see all that. The world will be unable to carry you then. The world will not be able to carry you then. The world and the 18,000 universes will become desperate in your presence. But if you do not receive this, you will have to carry the world, and you will become desperate. You have to understand this and keep this. This is for my true children. If they come on the right path, this is what I teach them. This is my personal wealth.

Truth & Light

WBAI Radio
New York

Sunday morning
December 16, 1973

LEX HIXON

This is Lex Hixon, and we have with us, this morning, Guru Bawa. This is the third time that he has come on the program, which is unusual. It has happened this way because he is a very, very unique being. Studio C is full of a lot of people. Guru Bawa is sitting facing us all, and we have been sitting quietly with him. And before we begin, I want to say a few things that I know of Guru Bawa.

From what I hear, some people in Ceylon used to make a regular pilgrimage that took them through a certain forest. And once or twice an old man kind of appeared to them, out of the forest. He noticed them, and they noticed him, and then he quickly disappeared again. And one time he stayed long enough for them to engage in a conversation. They felt a tremendous feeling of Light and Wisdom coming from him, and they asked if he would visit them sometime. They didn't know that this is, for Guru Bawa, the only way that he moves. When someone invites him someplace, he comes. So, a couple of weeks later, to their surprise, he turned up at the town where these people lived.

From there he gathered some students, and they moved to Jaffna. That was thirty years ago. Guru Bawa was an old man thirty years ago, and he looks like a young child today. I feel nothing coming from this man but the purest love of God, and he certainly makes me think of Sri Ramakrishna or Sri Ramana Maharshi, very much. He is a sage of the highest order, and thank heavens for this train of accidents or design that somehow brought him from an unknown, wandering being in the forests of Ceylon to this city, this country, and now this radio station today. It's quite remarkable that all of us have a chance to hear him.

But Guru Bawa is going back to Ceylon, we hear, in the next couple of months. Guru, we feel that we will be bereft of your presence and will feel kind of like children who are lost. Can you in some way give us a teaching that will sustain us when you are no longer with us physically?

GURU BAWA

My children, who are like my eye, my heart, my *Qalb*, my life, my Life within the life; my very, very precious children, who have mingled within the heart, within its life, in Love, I greet you most lovingly. It is the Truth that we have to speak of now. The heart does not separate and go away. The Truth does not separate and go away. Wisdom (Consciousness) does not separate and go away. The Commandment of God does not separate and go away. It will be mingled forever as the Heart within the heart. We know that very well. That has been my experience. The Truth never leaves a heart. The appearance of Wisdom and Truth will never

115

leave you. The Light of Truth, the Effulgence of Truth, the Truth of Wisdom exist within the children who are the Life within my life.

When Truth is in operation, that Truth will be known. The Truth of God is within all lives. It is intermingled in all lives. It constantly touches all lives. Since it is like that, and since the Light which is called Truth exists within us, there can be no separation.

Take the sun. When it rises, it shows us its light. There was a night section, then a light section. Although for the world it seems like night and then light, in itself the sun is always light. It is light on one side and light on the other side. When the world turns, then it is night.

It is like the mind. That is the night. The sun gives light for all 24 hours. It is the light for the world. But this aspect of the mind is the night. That is the aspect which is seen as the night without the light. For the aspect of Wisdom and for the aspect of Truth, the Light exists all the time. That is its Power. For all the 24 hours it shines within the heart. The Truth will never leave you. Therefore, there is no separation from my children. Only if God were separate from us would the Real Treasures be separate from us. Therefore, the children should not be sad about this.

There are about 1,500 letters that have come from Ceylon. The children are crying and crying. There is a famine and a lot of difficulties in that country. All of the things I predicted would happen, took place after I came here. They are begging and begging me to come again. There are certain things that are happening, and there are certain things that will still have to happen.

When you irrigate a rice field with water, the grass also grows. It grows there by itself. What can be done? We irrigate for rice, and grass also comes. What can be done? That is nature. The grass in the earth grows and tries to cover up the rice. You either have to weed the grass out or spray herbicides and kill the grass. Like that, a Guru, or one who knows the explanation, or one who has had experience—a farmer—will know what time the weeding should take place, and he will teach them to weed it out at that particular time. The more you weed, the better the crop will grow.

For those children in Ceylon, a lot of weeds have grown. We have to go there and weed a little and then come back here. If there are a lot of weeds which have grown here, then we will come to weed here a little and go back there.

LEX HIXON

Guru, this is the third time we have heard you speak, and we have had some preparation to understand you. Would you please pull all the weeds for us, right now? I mean, let's have a most powerful "thing".

GURU BAWA

Ah! My little brother, it is all there in nature. In the creation of God; there always are two kinds: the first is called the *zat,* and the other is called the *siffat.* One is called *khair,* and the other is called *sharr. Zat* is what is called Grace. That is of God's Grace—*Zat. Siffat* is called creation. God has created the creations. Then there is that called *sharr* and *khair. Khair* is good. *Sharr* is bad. These things have existed and these seeds have grown since the time when this earth was formed. When God started the process of creation with His Grace, when He took the earth part, these other things also crept in.

When water is taken to mix with the earth, there is an essence which exists in the water. When the air is taken to press with, there is an essence which exists in the air. When the fire is taken to heat with, there is an essence which exists in the fire. When the clay is heated and when paint is applied, there is an essence which comes with the paint, or the color. These weeds have come with this body even though God has created it with His Grace, which is known as Effulgence. If we pull these weeds this time, the next time we plow and sow and irrigate the field, the weeds will still come, even with the water itself.

Like that, there are qualities that come through our food. There are qualities that come with desire. There are qualities which come with bonds of affection. Then there are qualities which come with attachment to kinship. There are qualities which come with the mind. All of these weeds which come with the different ideas will be pulled up and will grow again. They will grow back. You have to pull the weeds again and again. Like this, if you pull the weeds before they mature and get seeds, before the weeds return and start flowering and bearing seeds, then the seed content of the weeds will be less. Little by little the number of weeds will be reduced until there are none left.

At that time, if you pull out the weeds with your Wisdom, then the One who watches the farm will have to come and pull out the weeds, too. The One who watches over the farm will have to come and weed also. If you go on weeding before the weeds blossom, little by little the weeds will become less in number. The weed seeds are here in this body. The children have to weed according to the way the Father teaches. If the weeding is done day by day, the number of weeds will be reduced. If the Father pulls out the weeds, and if you pull out the weeds, they will soon be gone.

LEX HIXON
Guru, what are we growing on this farm?

GURU BAWA
There are *khair* (the good) and *sharr* (the

119

evil). There is good food and there is bad food. We must pluck out the bad food. We must grow the good food. We can then give the good food to all lives. That is what must be grown. When a plant is known to be bad, it has to be pulled out immediately. Like that, all of the evil which is in the body has to be pulled out completely. We must grow the good food and give it to our brothers and sisters, to all lives. It has to be done like that. We have to do it like that.

There are wrong and right devotions to God, prayers, and searchings for God. These things have to be talked about a little. We must think about them a little. We have to think a little about how God can be seen. At a certain time that question came to Wisdom and was investigated. It was at the time when the Saints, and the Lights of God, and the 124,000 Prophets came to explain, at the time God told Moses to come to *Turshana* Mountain (that is what it is called in Arabic; in other scriptures it has been called Mount Sinai). The meaning of that is this:

God said, *"Ya Moses! You! Come up Mount Turshana! Come up Mount Turshana!"* The meaning is this: There is a mountain of desire by which we cause evil to others. The quality by which we abuse others, the quality by which we kill others, the quality by which we ridicule others, and 400 other qualities like

120

this, exist there. Moses is being commanded to discard those 400 evil qualities and to come above them. *"Come on top of the mountain! Come up Turshana Mountain!"* is what is said. Discard the concepts of "I" and "You" and come up. *"Come up Mount Sinai."*

"Sinai" means a dog. Desire. Attachment. Attachment to kin, connection to blood. So God was saying, *"Cut off these attachments and come up! Leave behind the Mountain of Turshana and come up. Leave desire and come up! Leave this dog and come! This dog is always licking, so leave it and come up! You have left Zahra, your wife, there. So leave her and come up. Leave the dog and the qualities of abusing others behind and climb up."* That was how it was told to Moses.

Like that, when we leave this place and go to communicate with God, if we want to go to God and to speak with Him, we must understand that Mount Sinai is this mind. We must climb above the mind. Desire is the dog that is at the pinnacle of the mountain. That is the place from which man falls. That is the place we must go beyond. Moses received the Ten Commandments there.

How did he see God? God is a Light. What he saw were the messengers from the seven heavens and that Light. Jesus saw God like that. Jesus saw that on Mount Sinai. Mohammed saw God like that. Abraham saw God like that.

Adam saw God like that. Noah saw God like that. Jonah saw God like that. Jacob saw God like that. David saw God like that. Joseph saw God like that. Job saw God like that. The Prophets communicated with God like that. What we have accepted is what those Prophets have told about. They said, "God has said this."

Right, my dear little brother, my dear children, what is it that came to them from God? It was Sound. It was Grace. It was Vibration. The Soul has no shape. It is Truth. That Power came to them. To whom did that Power come? It came to the Prophets. It is in them. What came from them? That Vibration. That Vibration comes from the Prophets. Where do those who want to receive that Vibration receive it? They have to receive it from this vibration—in the heart. This vibration will speak to that Vibration.

Without doing that, we have just made it into a book, a bible. That has a form. Or else we make it into a koran. That has a form. Or else we make it into a purana. That has a form. Those are all books. They all have form. If we are to receive that Vibration, we have to go within. Only if we go within can we understand the meaning of this. We have to think about this a little.

This form does not contain the meaning. We have to go within. We have to go within and look at that magnet. Having found the magnet, we have to establish the connection with it. If you go as a magnet and touch it, it will be attracted. Then there will be the recognition, "Ah!" This is it.

Like this, there is the wonder of God in our Life. What story does God have? Does He have wives? Does He have a history? Does He have children? What story, what history does He have? Is there a certain place, a Sacred City that He resides in? Is it written somewhere, "This is His Country"? Is there an historical document that says, "My God, the King, rules in this town at this place"? Does He have a form? Is there a statue of Him that can be seen by the eyes? Does He have a shadow? Can we point to the sun and say that is who He is? Can we point to the moon and say that is who He is? Can we point to the stars and say that is who He is? What is the proof, what is the basis for our worship? What is His story?

If you look at it from the viewpoint of proof, there is no story. There is no history. He has no form. He has no shape. How can we see Him? How can we worship Him? There is no story. We have to think about this a little.

My Father, where are You? There is no story. There is no dialogue. You have no form. You have no shape. There is no certificate that describes You. How can You be shown? We have to think about that.

He is not the earth. He is not the fire. He is

not the air. He is not the water. He is not the ether. They are all creations. These are the creations that God has created. There are many names for creation. Fire is there. He has created it. There is the sun. He has created it. There is the moon. He has created it. There are the stars. He has created them. The heavens are there. He has created them. There are the jinns and fairies and countless others that He has created. The reptiles, the birds, and all animals have been created by Him. He has created countless beautiful things. Thunder and lightning and fish have been created. His work of creation all has a form. The flowers exist, and they have so many colors. The colors exist. There are so many fruits, and the tastes exist. Sweetness and sourness exist.

This is all His creation. These are things that He made to be. We have to think about this a little. This (body) is the form. It is through this form that we have to discover His story. For God, there is no history. It is a mysterious thing. It is a thing which the mind and desire cannot see. It is a thing which is beyond mind and desire. We have to realize it with a higher Awareness. We have to be aware of it.

We also have to think about this a little: When we say "God," what is it? Some people have made a dog into a god. Some have made a fish into a god. Some have made a cat into a god. Some have made a rat into a god. Some have made a snake into a god. Some have made a cow into a god. Some have made a horse into a god. Some have made a donkey into a god. Some have made a rooster into a god. And some have made a crow into a god.

Like this, all the creations in the world have been made into gods. Some people have made fire a god, some have made the sun a god, some have made the moon a god, some have made the stars into gods. Some people have made the earth a god, some have made the water a god, some have made the air a god, some have made fire a god, and some have made the ether into a god. Some have made all the colors into a god. These are all creations. This is what is called creation. How can creation be turned into God? How can we call it God? How can we ask it for favors? This is what we have to think about. We have to accept real Wisdom. From that we have to know the explanation. We have to be aware of that Truth. We have to see what kind of Treasure it is. If we study this Wisdom, if we understand this Wisdom, then we can see our Father.

He has no mantra. All the mantras are for creation. All the mantras are for birth. They are not His mantras. He is a different Treasure.

If we want to understand Him, we must do it in this way: As we are looking, if we see a snake, then we must examine that. How many colors does it have? When it catches the sun, how many colors does the snake show? Ah, it has poison in its mouth. It dances beautifully, but it can kill with a glance. It will come to sting very fast. You say, "Oh God, You have created this beautiful snake and You have also created poison in it. You have enabled it to dance. As I dance to the snake, it will dance to me. Ah, what a wonder! What a wonder your creation is!"

If you look at a flower—this is His story. Creation, itself, is His story. Whatever creation there is exists as His history. Whatever flower He has made exists as His history. Every section that He has created, He has made within it: its Truth, its qualities, the consciousness of it, the understanding of it, the research into it, and the praise of it. "My God! What wonder exists!"

He has created a fruit and its taste. You say, "Ah, what a taste! My Father!" We have to inquire into everything. When we accept the lessons that can be drawn from it, it is God Himself who must be praised. You say, "Ah, my God!" Whatever explanation we come to know, when we accept it and see it with Wisdom, it is God whom we are praising.

When we investigate the earth, there are gems within it. There is oil within it. There is fire burning within it. There is sulfur in it. There is mercury in it. There are currents in it. There is magnetism in it. There are nine kinds of precious gems within it. There is Light within it, and there is a value within that which is beyond any estimate. There is energy within it. Finally, we say, "Ah, what a wonder, what a wonder—Your history! Who else could create but You? What beauty!"

You see some food and you taste it. You say, "Ah, what a wonder Your wonder is!" If you look at the sun, the rays, the light, you say, "Ah, what a wonder, what a wonder! You can make the oceans into valleys and the valleys into oceans!"

Like this, everything that is seen has His story within. He is a Mechanic. He is an Artist. He is a Scientist. He is a Psychologist. He is a Doctor. He is a Worker in the "shaker-maker" company. It is like this. He is a Master. He is a *Gnani* (One who is Divinely Wise). He is a King. He is a Poet. He is One Who Knows. He is a

Beggar. He is a Rich One. He is a Slave. Like this, He does so many things. We have to know His work.

If we are to understand Him, we must realize His story, and that He has created His story. Whatever has been born, if you take the Truth within it and if you look at it, you will say, "My God!" If we do this with each thing that comes, then it is He, Himself, who is there. His story is there. His abilities are there. He Himself exists forever. Everything else is the story, the things which have been born out of Him.

They are things which are subject to agreement. We have to study and know Him through these "books". We have to realize Him through these "words". He is showing His Treasures through these Lights. The One Treasure comes like this. All the rest change and come back again. They grow again. They are sowed and then they are reaped. They come like this. He is the only One who is Alone like that. This is a mystery. Whatever we see has come with a form. He has created His story within it. If you look at each story, and if you look at each speech, then it is all a wonder. It is all a wonder. If all the wonders in all the creations—in the birds, in the green things, in all creations—are combined, that is the history of the Father. None of these is equal to that. This is History. Each thing is an example.

He created a cow. That is an example. He created an elephant. That is an example. He created the sun. That is an example. All the Power for these examples is in His hand. That is a mystery. That has no form. That is a thing which cannot be seen. The praise for all of this belongs to Him. *"Alhamdullillah!"* That is an Arabic word: "It is all You. Everything." When Wisdom comes to someone, and as he goes on researching, God Himself exists as God. All the rest is His history. They are His storybooks. Whatever has been created is a book. That has a form. It may have a form. It may have beauty. It may have color. It may be wood. It may be a flower. It may be food. It may be a taste. When you taste everything, what do you ultimately see? Truth. The Truth and the taste. What is that? That is God.

Other than that One Treasure, everything else is a *puranam* (scripture). They are His *puranam,* His creation. They are all stories through which to see Him. We have to know Him through these. He has to be known through the explanation of His creation. He has to be known through each vibration of each explanation, through Wisdom, and through His Qualities. Understanding this, if we see, then we will know there is no one other than He. Nothing is equal to Him. Nothing is at the same place He is. He has no opposite; nothing is like Him. He was not born; He does not die. It is a Treasure that cannot be destroyed. It is a Treasure which exists forever.

It is a Treasure which is forever within all lives. It is a Treasure which is intermingled in everything. It is an essence which is manifested. It is a Taste. It has to be understood and learned from each taste. Although we have to understand Him through each of these, they are not God. There is no comparison to God. There is no room for us to worship anything else. There is no place for us to chant to any of these other things.

God is God. All we can do is say, "Ah, my God, what praise, what praise! My God!" What we must do is praise Him and go on. We must praise Him, we must reflect upon Him, we must taste Him, we must taste His Truth. Other than this, what else can be? He is there. There is nothing else. We must understand this story. We can see God through this.

We can research into atoms. We say, "Ah, You gave so much power to this atom! What wonder! What wonder! You are an Atom within this atom. When I do research on this atom, You are inside the atom. Have You stopped at the atom? Have You gone beyond the atom to the un-atom? What a wonder! Ah, what a wonder! What a taste!" We have to understand each thing like this.

We study science. We think this is a new study. It is a small lesson in what Man has to learn. In the creation of God, science is a small lesson. Man's birth is a lesson. His fetus is a lesson. Where he was before is a lesson. Where he has come to now is a lesson. Where he is going is a lesson. His death is a lesson. What he has to know is a lesson. Seeing his Father is a lesson. Understanding it is a lesson. Knowing and understanding the taste is a lesson. Among all these lessons, science is a small lesson. All these lessons are within him. He has to open the book.

God's Secret, His Mystery, His *Zat* (Essence), and His *siffat* (creation), are all within Man. Having created all of these creations, He rolled all of them into what is called man, or Man-God, God-Man. He placed all His Secrets inside man. This "book" we call man is a very big book. If you investigate this book, inside it there is ignorance. There is false wisdom. There is the darkness which is called illusion—torpor. There is Satan, and also there is God inside. The earth is inside. The "Red Sea" is inside. The seven oceans are inside it. The seven *nafs* (evil qualities) are inside it. These are the seven *nafs* with which you tell lies. And the seven states of consciousness with which you know God are inside this "book". The Truth is within it. Hell is within it. And heaven is within it. God's Grace and His *Rahumath*—His limitless Wealth—are within it. The 18,000 universes are within it.

If a man understands who he is, then he will know who God is. If he knows who God is, he will know God's kingdom. To whom does

131

this kingdom belong? It belongs to One who can be called the "Sun" of God. What is the kingdom of God? Each heart is the kingdom of God. In every creation He has created the *Qalb* (heart), which is the kingdom of God. His kingdom exists in His countless creations. And this vast kingdom is the Central Place. His Throne exists within the kingdom of all that He created with the resonance of *"Allahoo,"* and all that He raised with the *"hoom"* (the primal resonance). That is the kingdom of God. One who understands what the kingdom of God is, is the Sun of God. That is the "Sun," not the "son". It is not this form. It is the Light—His Light. That Light is known as the Sun. One who understands the kingdom of God is the Sun—that Light. God has no form. What does He have? Light. He has His Power. That Power is His Sun. That is Light. He has no form, and He cannot have a son like that. That Light is called the Sun. That Grace is what is called the Sun.

The snake has poison. If you love the snake and become like a snake, eventually that snake will give you poison. The Treasure which God has is Light. And if you love God, then He will give you His kingdom—Light! That is what He will give. That is what He says. In everything that He has created, it is His kingdom. That kingdom exists in everything. It is there in the atom. If not for God, not even an atom would move. Nothing can move—none of the moving things can move—without the Grace of

God. They cannot move without His Power. A Light has that same kind of Power.

All the created things that move have shadows. All of the things which have shadows eventually change. That shadow has an agreement. That form has an agreement. It exists for a certain time, then it changes and becomes some other form. This is what we have to understand. This form is not God. This shadow is not God. If this is understood, then it will be understood that He has placed the kingdom of God in each of His created beings. In everything that He has created, He has created what is called the *Qalb*, or heart. His kingdom is within the heart. We have to understand that kingdom. If we understand His kingdom, then we will understand that we are not the earth, fire, water, air, or ether.

The Soul is the Treasure that came from God. He says, *"That is my Trust."* He has placed that in the kingdom of God. It is because of His help that His Grace continues. That Treasure of Grace is the Sun of God. Man-God. If you look at both, they will not be different. This is a Light, and that is a great Resplendence. This "sun" will go and disappear into that "Sun". Then "you" and "I" are nothing. We are all the *puranas* of His history. His explanations. His aspects. This is what we have to understand, my children who are like gems within my eyes, this is what we have to understand. This is the Truth. It is this One Treasure whom we call

God. It is through this Treasure that we must know Him and go to His Place. We must go to the inside of everything we see.

When you take a gem out of the earth, you won't see the light within the gem at first. You have to cut off the common rock and the imperfections. As you go on cutting and faceting, the hidden beauty within will emerge. At that time, the value of the gem will increase. Then it will be given a value. That is nature. Like that, my little brother, this Sun of the gem which is known as the Truth, that resonance of God which is known as the Truth, is here. That Sun of God is here. The earth, fire, water, air, ether, Satan, hell, all cover it and conceal it. The demons and the jinns and the fairies and *maya* (illusions) are all covering it. They are covering it (that Sun) because it grew within them. That is creation. It has grown within the earth, fire, water, air, and ether. The Truth is inside. That is where the Sun of God is. We have to accept that Light.

What do we have to do? We have to cut with Wisdom. We have to cut in four directions. We have to cut and measure four sides. We have to separate them and say, "This side is the east side, this side is the west side, this side is the north side, this side is the south side." When all of these have been cut off, then the Light, the Original Light within, will come out. Then, from any side that you look at the gem, the Light will be seen. "Ah, here is my God, here is my God, here is my God, here is my God!" No matter what side is looked at, this Light will be known. No matter what side is turned, the Light will be seen. That Power will be known.

Like this, we have to cut off and discard the coverings. When all the things that are closing off the Light are discarded, then we will see the Light that is called Man-God, God-Man. All the things that are closing off the Light have to be cut and cut again. It is Wisdom which has to see this. We have to think, "God is not this light nor this—this is all creation. We cannot accept the sun or the moon or any of the other things. They are all things which have an agreement. When their time comes, they will go."

In the Tamil *puranas,* there is a book called *Thirrukural.* It tells about Shivan wearing the crescent of the moon on his head. And in certain religions some people worship Shivan as a God. Now science has gone beyond the moon. The scientists have gone beyond the moon, and they have stood on the moon. So, if the moon is on the head of Shivan, and the scientists are on the moon, then Shivan is below the scientists.

Shivan was wearing the crescent on his head, and the scientists have gone above the crescent. So fortune-telling and horoscope-casting are below that, and finished. Now

135

Shivan is also below. The scientists have gone above him. If the scientists have gone above the crescent, how can we call that God? It was only an example. The explanation is available to the *Gnani* (One who is Divinely Wise). We cannot worship the crescent or stories. There is a greater Treasure. Within man, there are 70,000 suns. Within a man, there are 70,000 moons. Within a man, there are countless stars.

If at one time there is good luck, a person might say, "Oh, this is a good star for me. This is a good star." He is a "star" on the stage. This is an act. You cannot find God with this star. It is not this. If we examine this through Wisdom, we will know the difference. The *puranas*, the scriptures, show external things. They are all examples. The *puranas* were sung at a certain time. Poets sang the *puranas*, and they showed examples.

There is a period of time called "Ammavaseh"— the dark of the moon— when the moon cannot be seen. One time, a man looked and did see it. At first, he saw only a line. Then he looked harder and said, "There is something there." He tried to show it to someone. He said, "Look at that. Look straight above that tree. Look, see that branch. Now, see that leaf on that branch. Now, look beyond that. Look straight at the leaf, then above it, and there you will see that line." He showed all the other things in order to show the moon.

Like the tree, these words are all examples. We have to go inside them to see. These are just examples. These are all examples. We say, "It is under that. Look within that. Look under that, under that. It is like that; it is like that." Whatever we see, everything that we see, is an example. The meaning is within. If we go on cutting and cutting and cutting and go within it, the meaning will be there. Then the meaning will be understood. Then the Power within will be understood. "Ah, that is the wonder!"

My little brother, we have to accept each explanation. "Oh, what a wonder this world is!" There is something called *Gnanam* (Divine Wisdom). If each breath praises God, that is *Gnanam*. Accept that. When you think about it and see it with your Wisdom, then you will say, "Oh God, oh my God, all praise belongs to you." This thought and this intention will go to Him. Each and every word will go to Him. Every word and every breath will praise Him. Each breath will continue to praise Him. How could He leave us and go? How could He be far away from us? When every word is His Word, how can He leave us? This is prayer. This is worship. All praise belongs to Him. This is the way we have to become.

It is not to see all these outer lights and this and that. From His Place, the rain of His *Rahumath* (His Grace) has come here. Later, the rain will evaporate and go back to the heavens. It will return as rain. The rain is pure, without the salt from the sea. It provides benefit to all. It bathes all the vegetables and the flowers and the fruits. The water that remains goes back into the ocean. Which is the rain that falls? Which is the water that was there before? Of the water that fell into the ocean, how can it be said, "This is my water, and that is the water that belongs to the ocean?" Which is mine, and which water belongs to the ocean? Can we separate the rainwater from the sea water? Is it separable? It can't be done. It is all the same. It is like that. It is one. You can't say, "This is my rain." You can't take it out like that.

Like the rain, this is the way that God and His Light and what is called His *"Rahumath"* have set down the Soul of Man. He has placed the Soul here in creation. Man has come here to understand His story. Man has to understand the story of God. Who has created me? Who is my Father? What is His Beauty? What is His shape? What is He like? We have to learn our Father's story. We have to study His wonders. We have to accept His Explanation. As we study His story, His history, and His *purana,* we have to do this with His Qualities. Patience, Tolerance, Forbearance, Peacefulness, Compassion, Love, Generosity, Kindness, Charity, Open-heartedness, Justice, Conscience, and Truthfulness have to be taken within us. It has to be done through these Qualities.

138

These are the Qualities of God. They are the Trust of God. They are the City Government. They are the Treasury. What do they do in the City Government Building? They give licenses and deeds and explanations. That is the municipal government. City Hall. Our City Hall is His Quality. For His kingdom, what is called City Hall is His Quality. His Love, His Goodness, His Beauty. When we describe that Quality in that City, He absorbs that description, and says, *"My son, my child!"* He falls into the *Qalb* and He absorbs it into Himself. *"Ah!"* It is His Justice, His Truthfulness, His Scripture, and He is happy and He absorbs it and embraces it and says, *"My son!"* He falls into that ocean which is known as the *Qalb*—He falls into that City—and He absorbs it.

He falls into the City and He embraces it and says, *"You are my son. Go into the world and help all lives. You have been truly born to me. Grow my Grace. Grow all lives with that Love."*

God says that, and the rain of Grace returns. That *Rahumath* which is known as the Wisdom, the Treasure, the Compassion, and the Love, falls again. As it falls, it gives Feeling to some; it gives the flowers and the trees taste. It is like that. There is no "I" for that. It came and fell into the ocean. It exists there in contentment. That is not "I". That is not the rain. That is He. Only if you can separate it, can it be two. But it can't be separated. God has mingled with God. God's Treasure is with God. God exists as God, conversing with God. God helps God.

That is the way, little brother. That is *Gnanam.* How can we separate that? What is there to say, "I saw" about? What is there to say, "I spoke" about? There is nothing about which you can say, "I am that" or "I am this". That is that. God is God. It has come from Him, and it is given back to Him. It goes back into God. This is the way. This is the way the Truth is. We have to think about this a little. It is easy to say, but to act according to it is difficult. We have to know this well; we have to see this Explanation with Wisdom.

If you take an atom, my little brother, and if you cut it into ten million pieces, and if you take one of those particles and examine it, you find that there are 99 atoms inside that particle—revolving around without touching each other. If you take one of those 99 atoms, and if you cut it into a thousand particles, and if you take one of those particles, you will see 99 atoms revolving within that particle without touching each other. If you take one of those 99 atoms, and if you cut it into 600 particles, you will find 99 more atoms revolving around without touching each other. Then, if you take one of those particles, and if you cut it into 100 particles, you will find 99 atoms revolving around without touching. If we take that particle and look at it, then our Wisdom will have gone into that. It has been totally absorbed into that.

This 99 is His. Creation, His Abilities, everything is His. The 99 is not finite. It is infinite. Yet, there is One, a hundredth one in His hand, that gives it Completion. That explanation comes. In all your investigations into science or anything else, until you understand God, you see only more of His wonders and His mysteries without end. He is in the one-hundredth name—the Power of creation, sustenance, and absorption. In that One, He contains the Power to manifest creation, to protect it and sustain it, and the Power to ask it to come back—to summon it, to question it, and to pass judgment. I am nothing. *La-ilaha*, I am nothing. *Il Allahoo*, You are God. Until the "I" disappears into that realization, no investigation can ever reach Completion.

When you say, "It is You, O God," and when you disappear into Him, then that is what exists. That is what is. Nothing else. I am nothing. Only God exists. God is God. It is like that. That is the way we have to do our research. We have to accept this explanation. We are going to see wonders while understanding this kind of circumstance. There is no end to it. This is what we call our Father. That is what we call Him. This is the wonder.

LEX HIXON

Guru Bawa, thank you very much. Guru Bawa, is this Gem that is Guru Bawa—has the process of cutting that gem become complete now?

GURU BAWA

I'm still cutting. Still measuring. There is a lot to learn. I am a student. I am learning.

LEX HIXON

For the benefit of the people listening at home, really the best part of these mornings comes, in some way, after the talk when we go off the air and everyone who is here receives an embrace from Guru Bawa. You can't see that on the radio, but he takes people into him. He takes his own Qualities into himself, by embracing them. I know that he himself or his disciples are too discreet to really plead with people to come to see him. But I, personally, am absolutely shameless. I will plead with people to come to see Guru Bawa. He is a gem, a priceless gem.

About "God's Funny Family"

Guru Bawa often refers to his "children" (members of the many Guru Bawa Fellowships in the United States and his disciples in Ceylon) as "God's funny family." Indeed, until Wisdom comes, we are often as funny as fish looking for water.

To help our wisdom grow, Guru Bawa has created the Fellowships as reservoirs from which those thirsting for Truth can drink that pure water of clarity. We invite you to share our cup. Write to the Guru Bawa Fellowship, 5820 Overbrook Ave., Philadelphia, Pa., for locations in other cities.

Also available by Guru Bawa

Paperbacks:
    The Divine Luminous Wisdom That Dispells
        the Darkness—Man-God, God-Man . . . . .
    Songs of God's Grace . . . .

Magazine:
    God's Light . . . .   10 issues

Cassette Recordings:
    WBAI Interview, Oct. 14 . . . .
    KQED Interview, Oct. 27 . . . .
    Songs of God's Grace (vol. 1-4) . . . . ea.

Videotapes:
    Please contact the Guru Bawa Fellowship of Philadelphia for information.